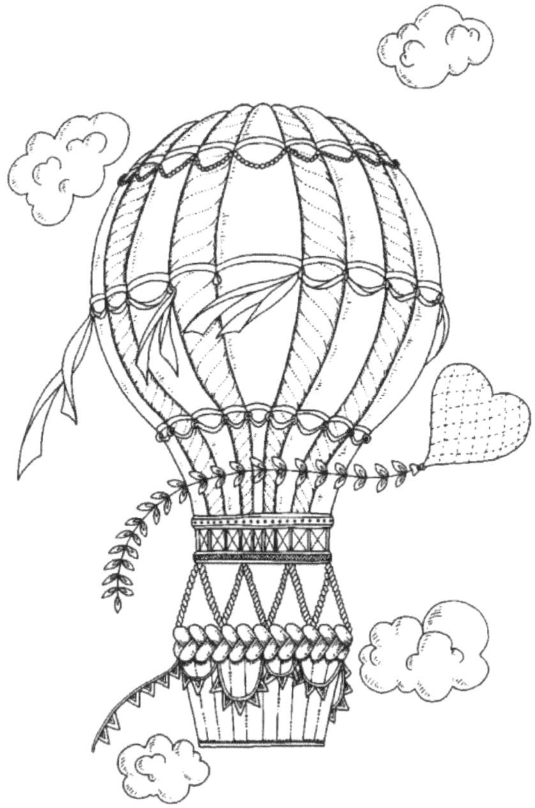

BALLOON PUBLISHING

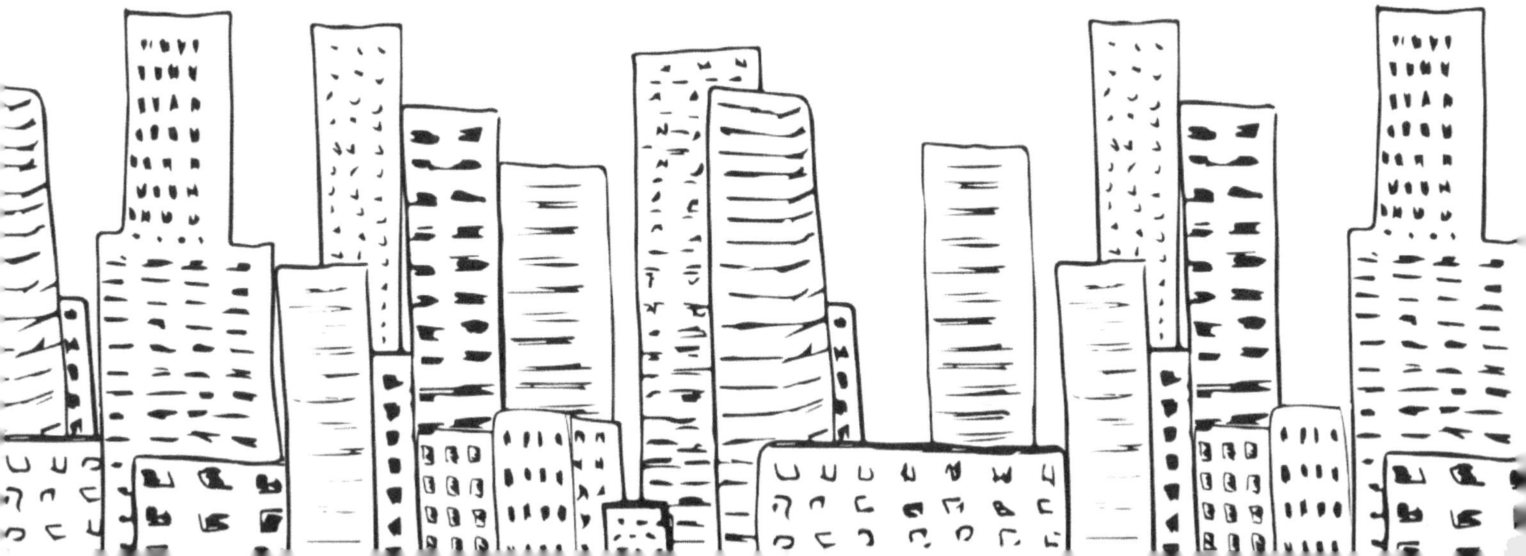

COLOR TEST PAGE

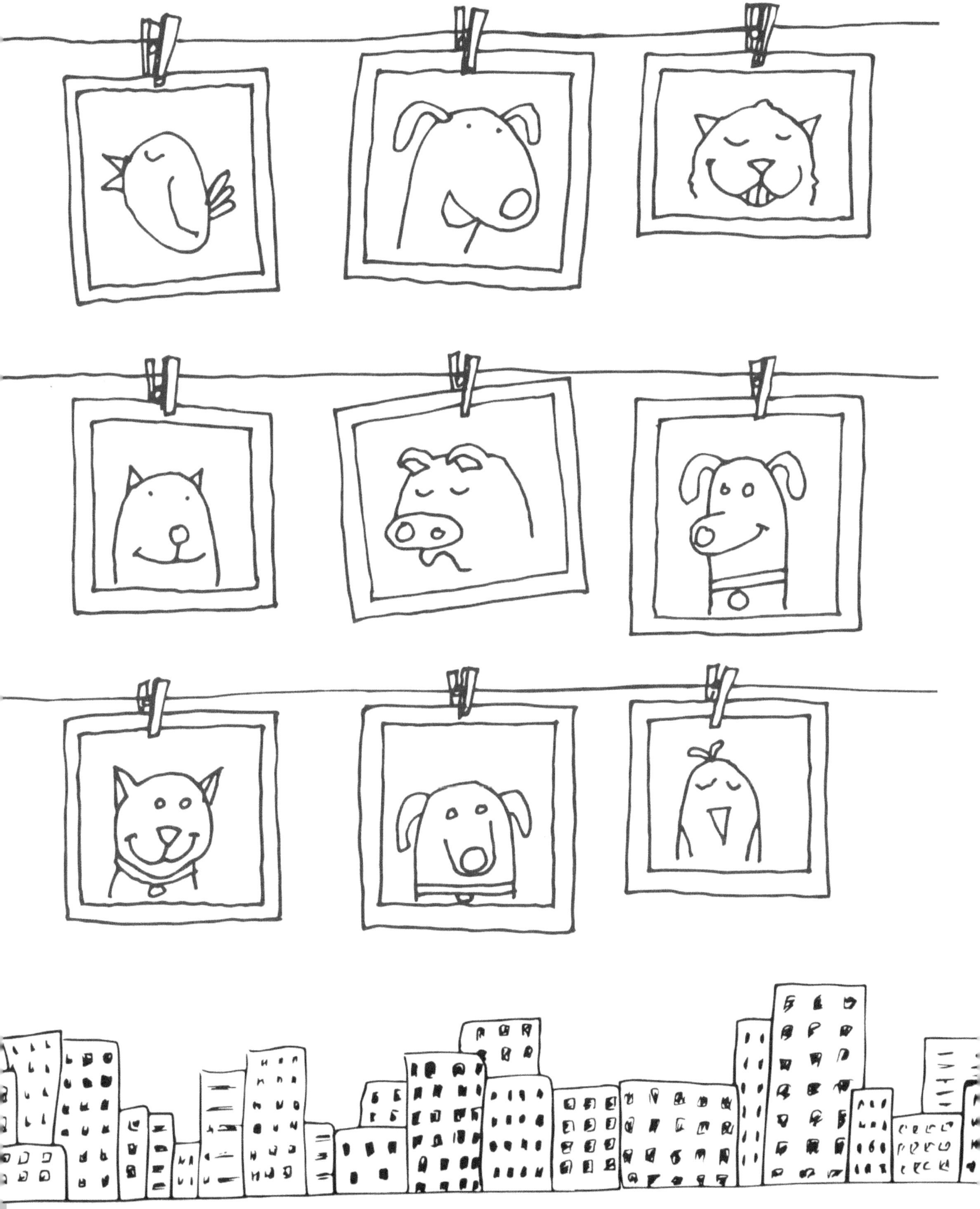

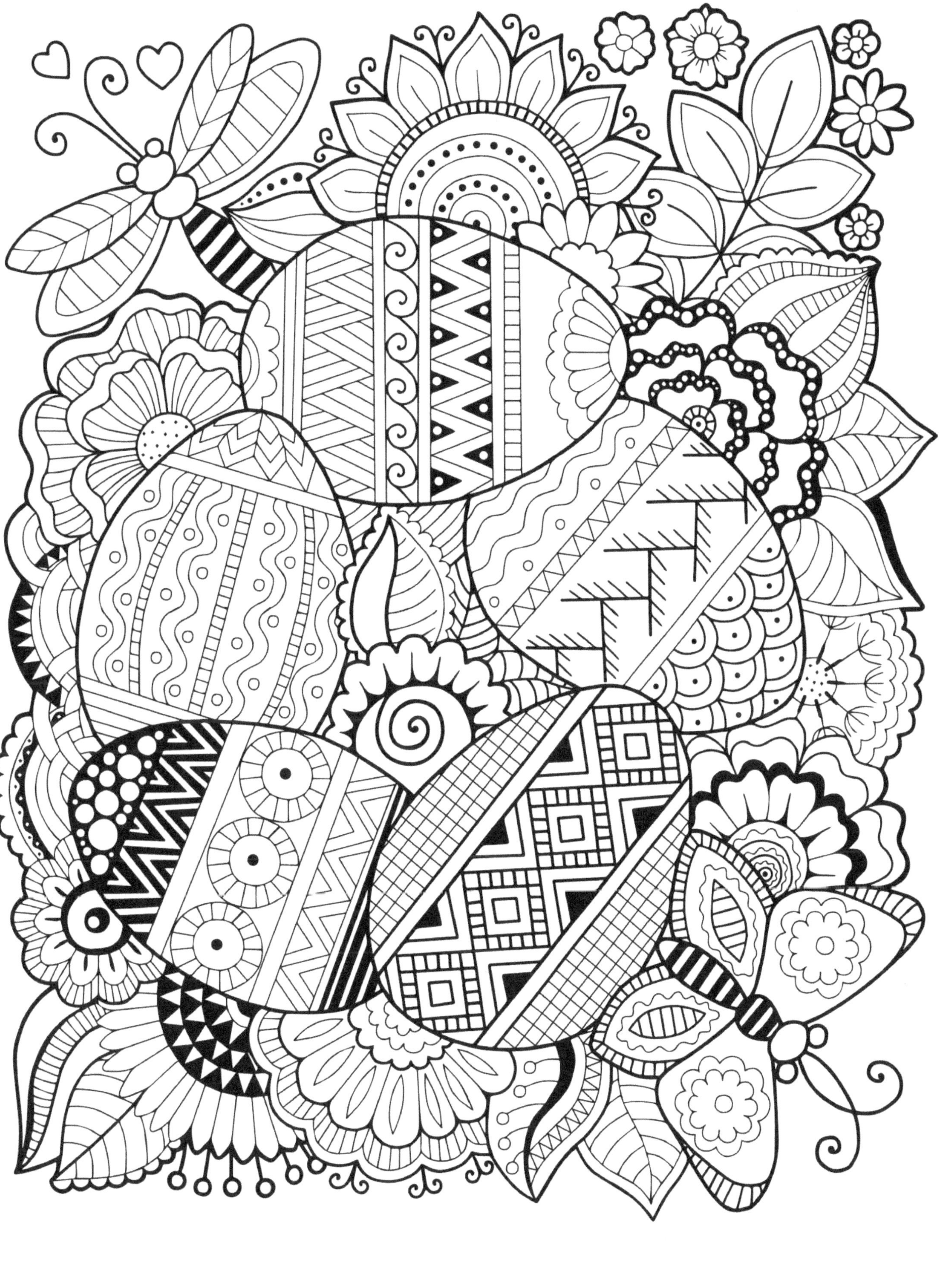

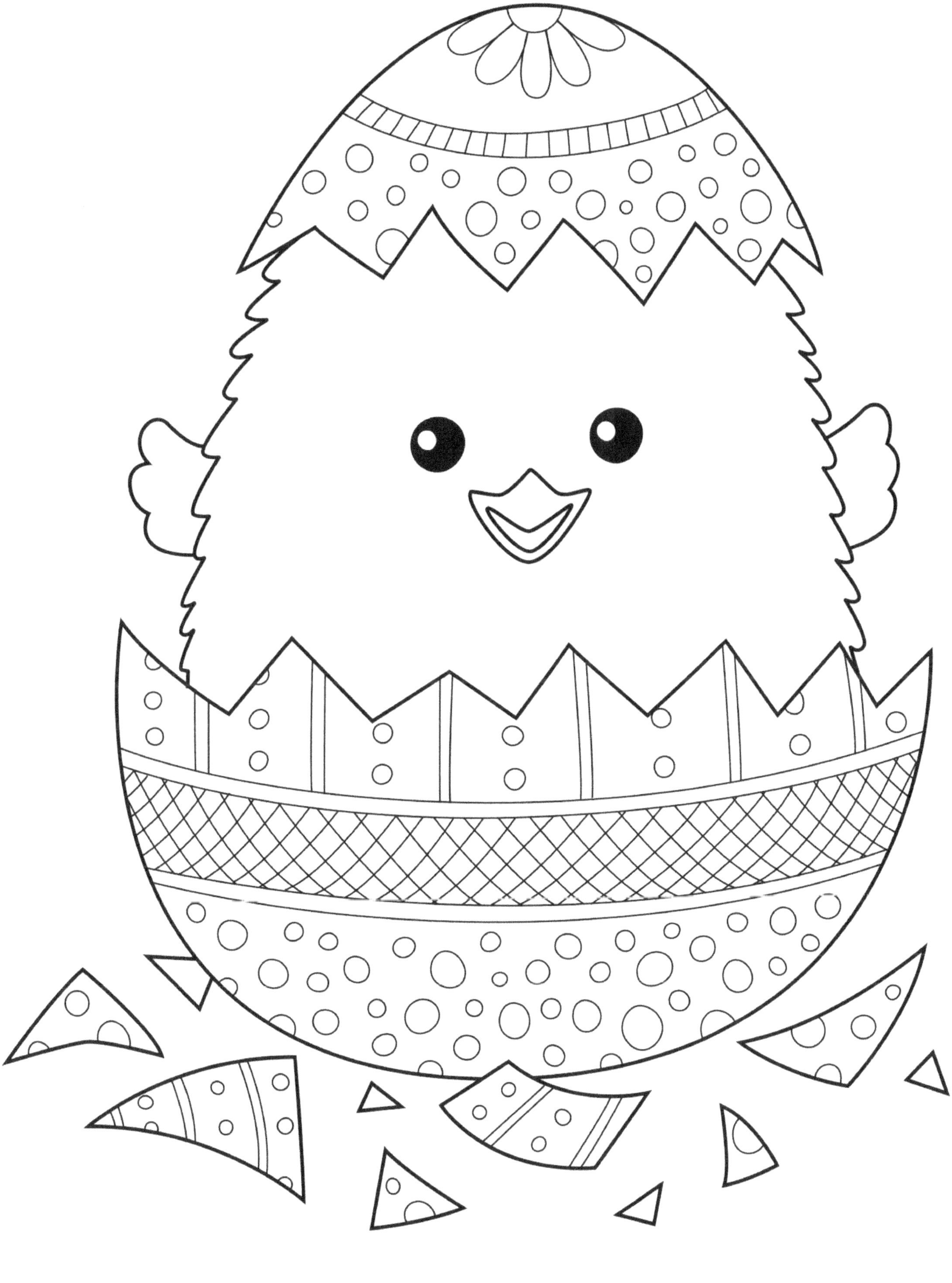

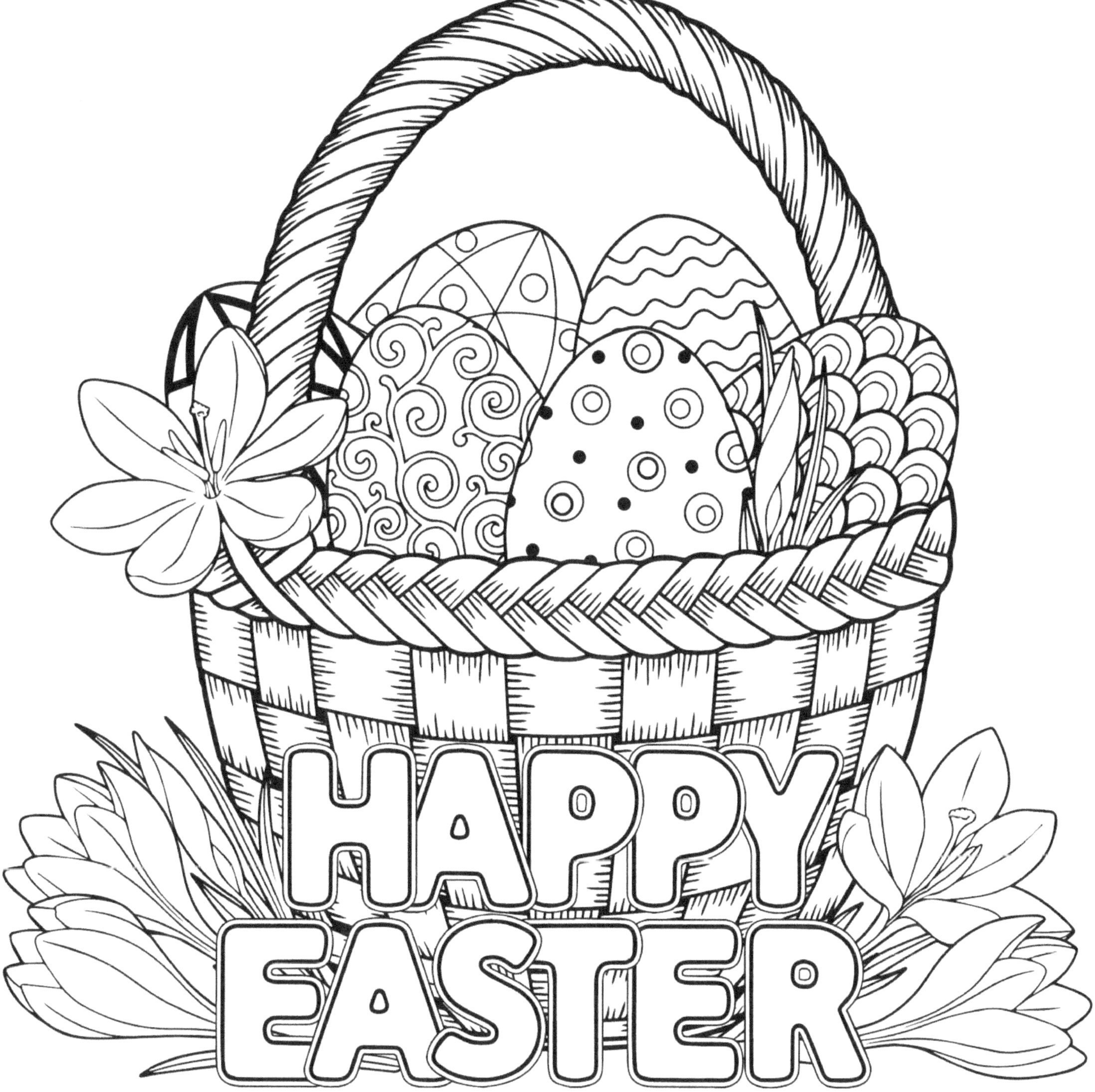
HAPPY
EASTER

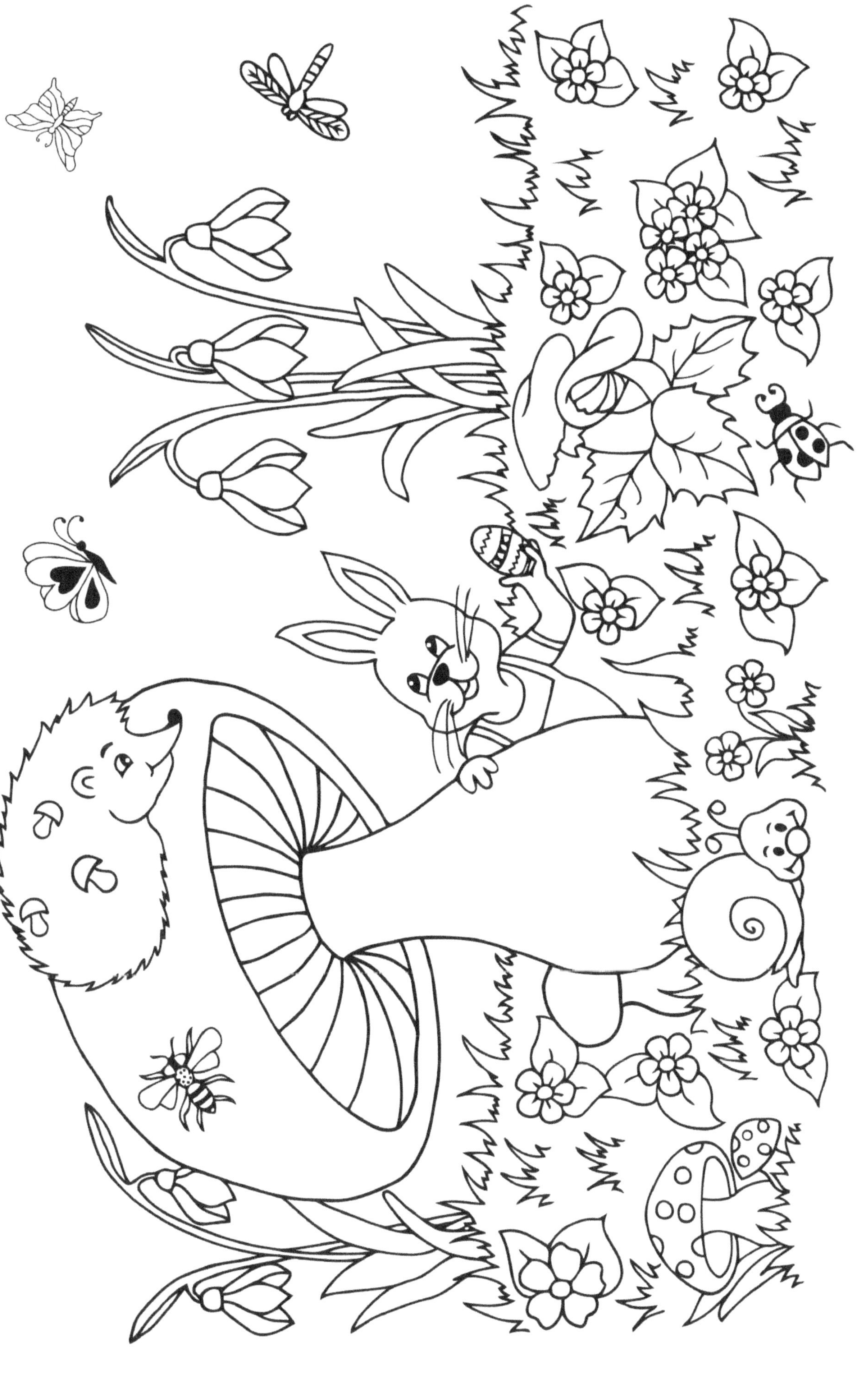

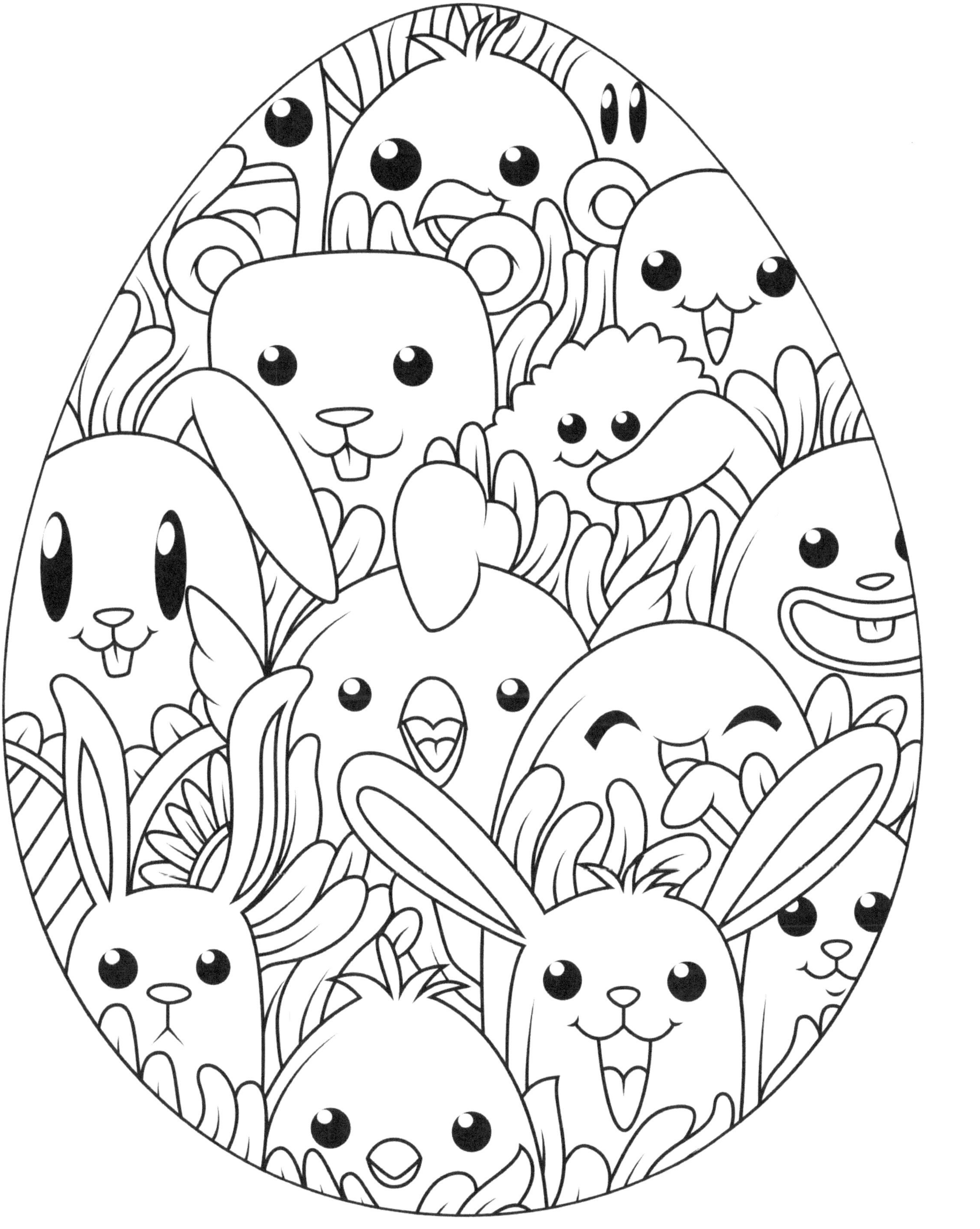

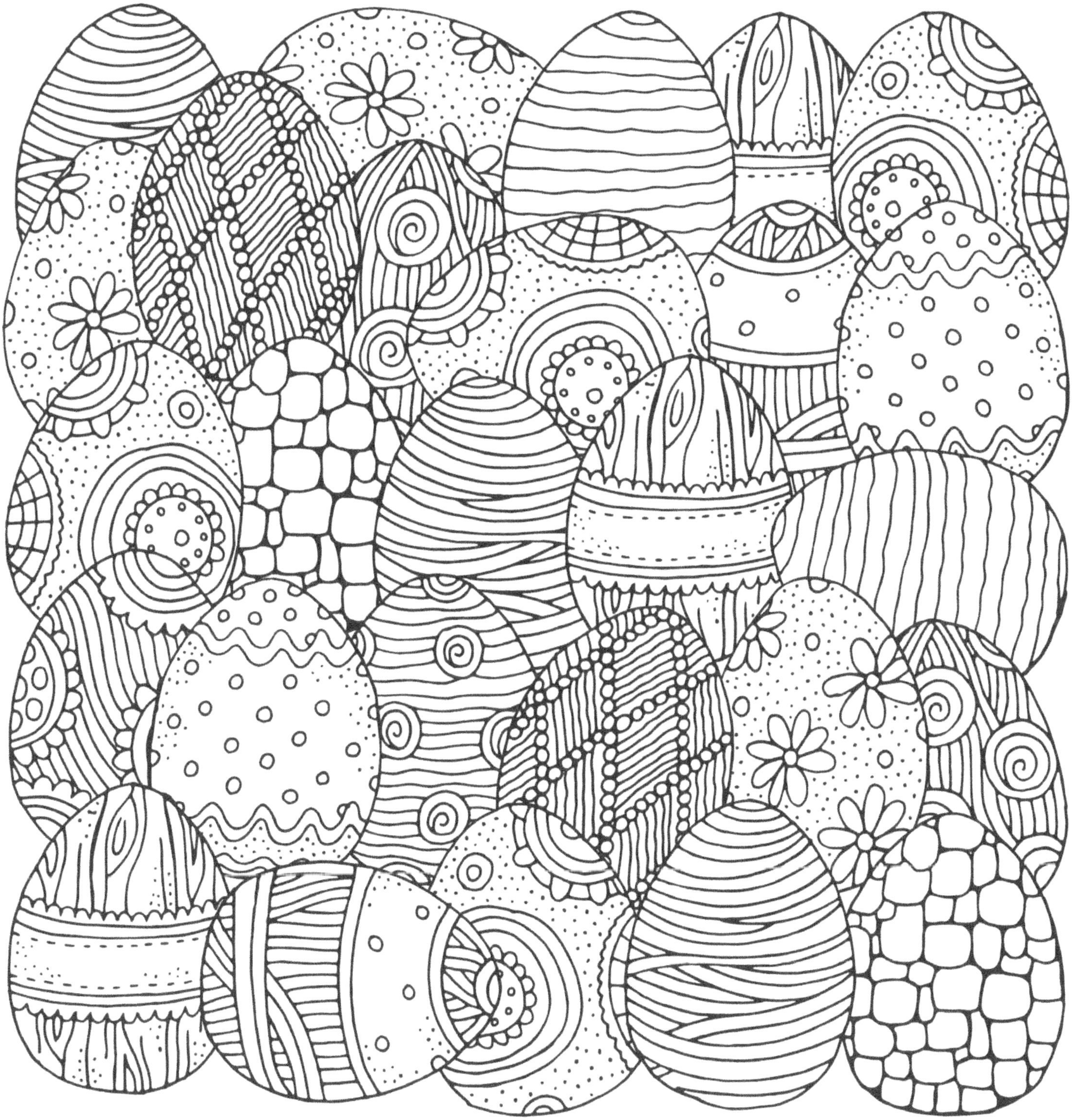

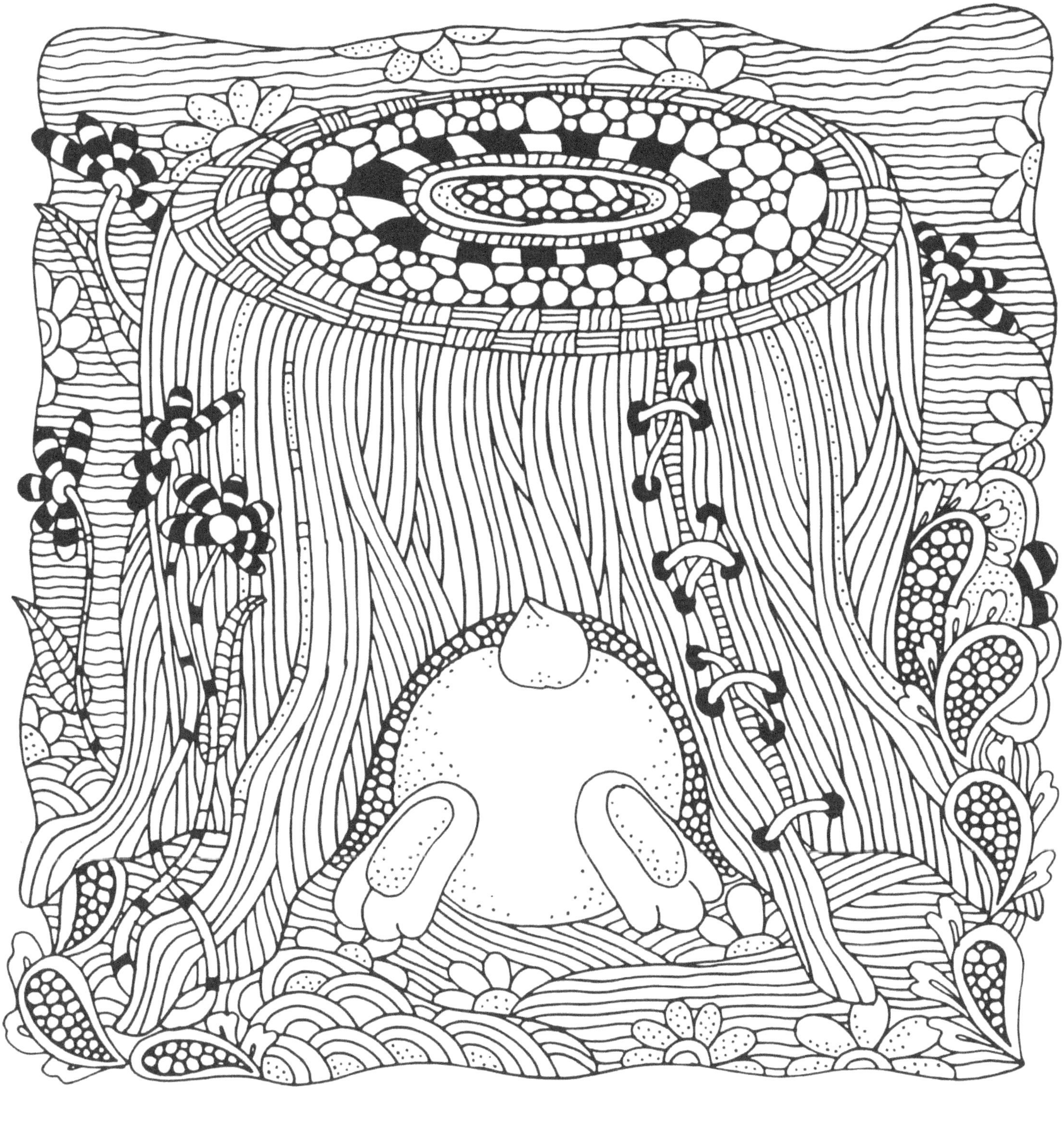

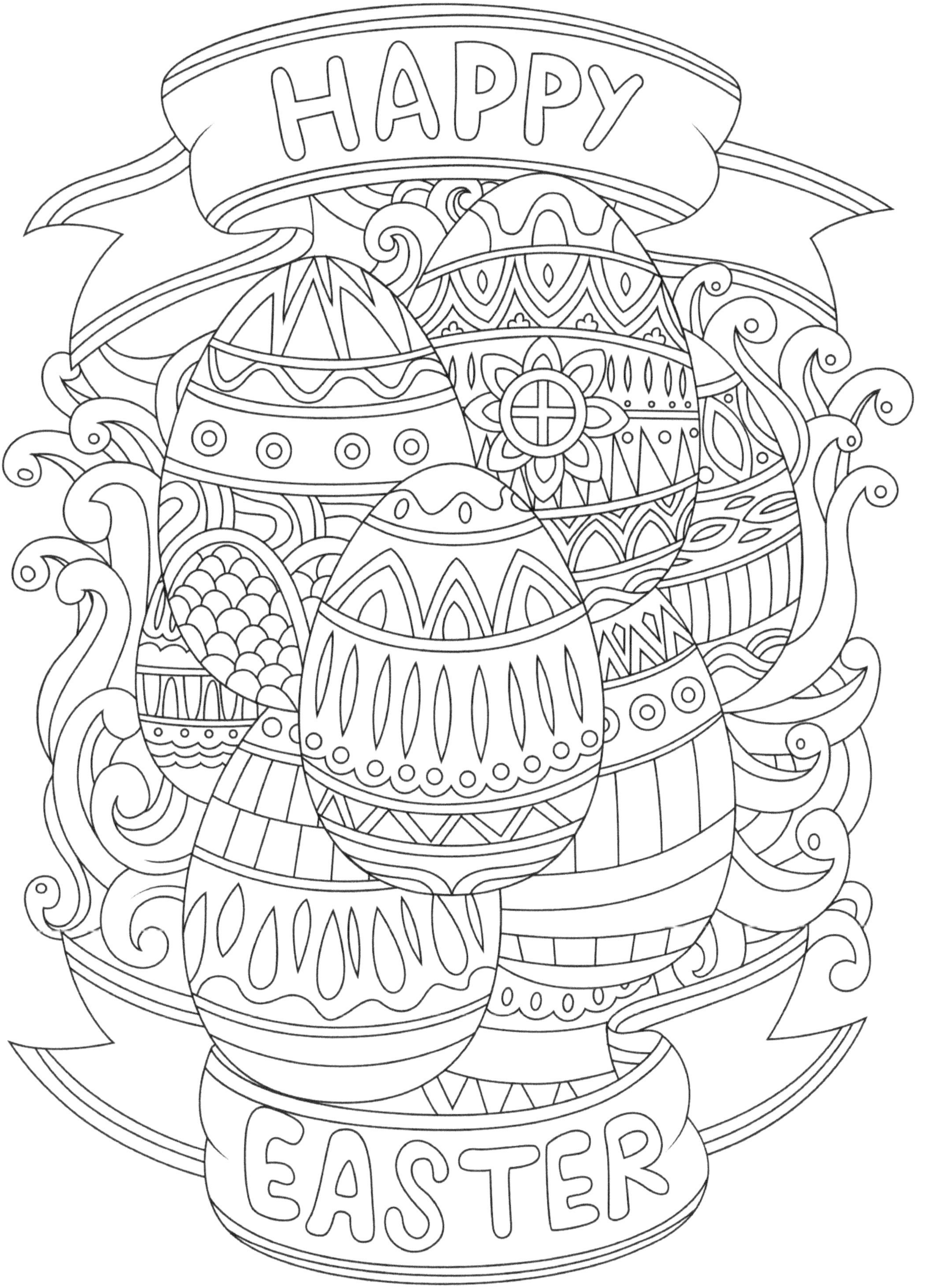
HAPPY
EASTER

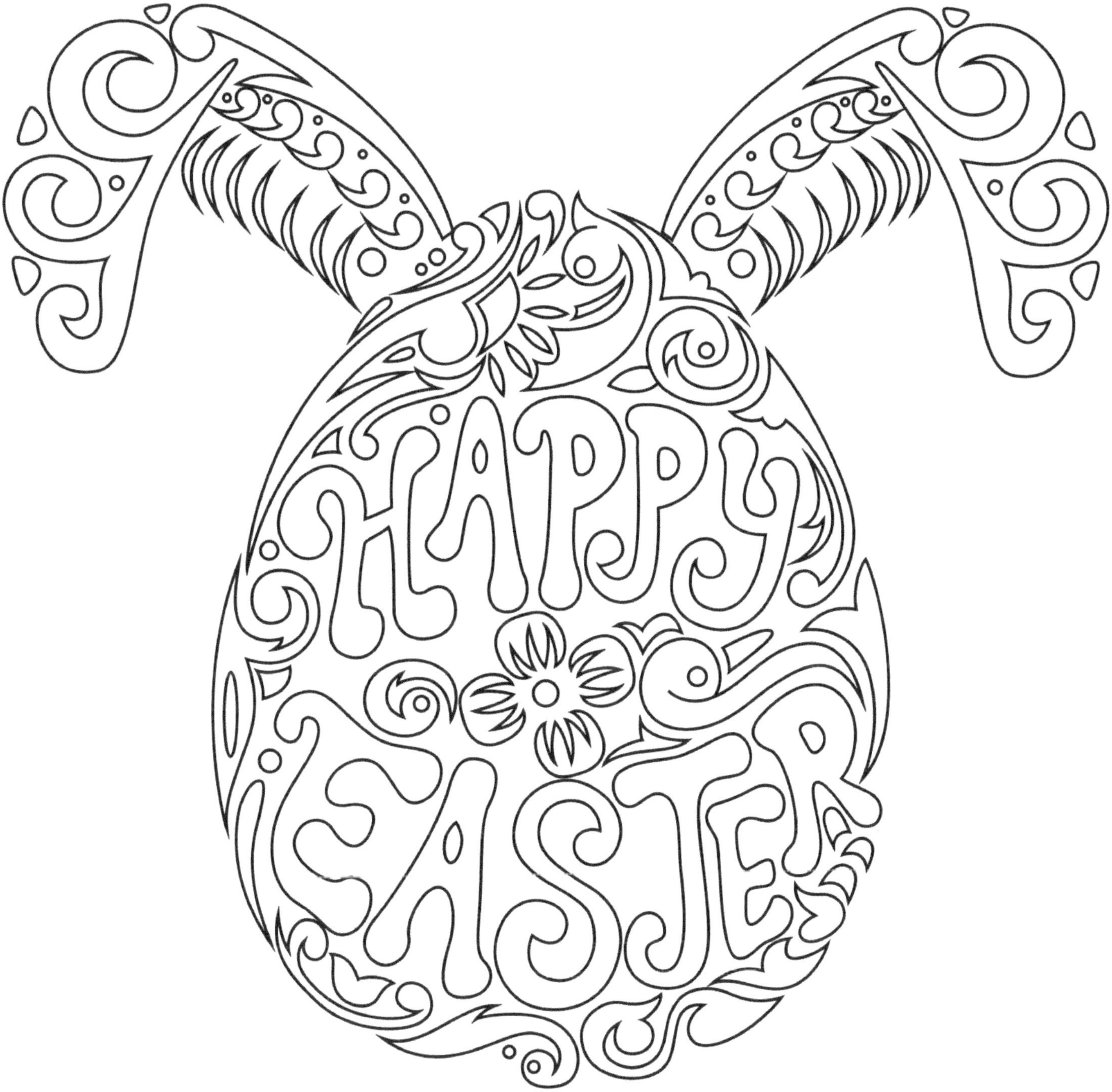
HAPPY
EASTER

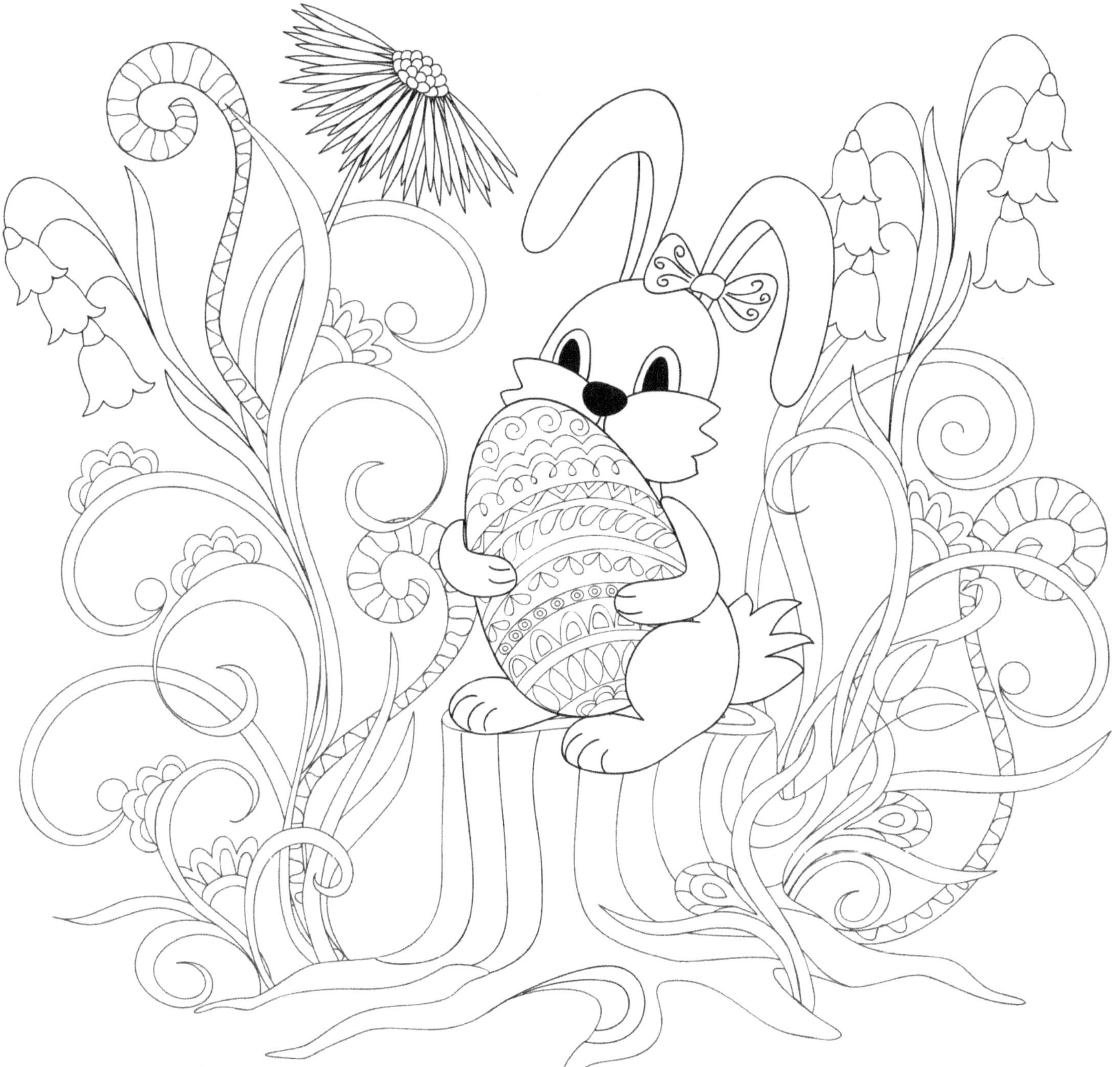

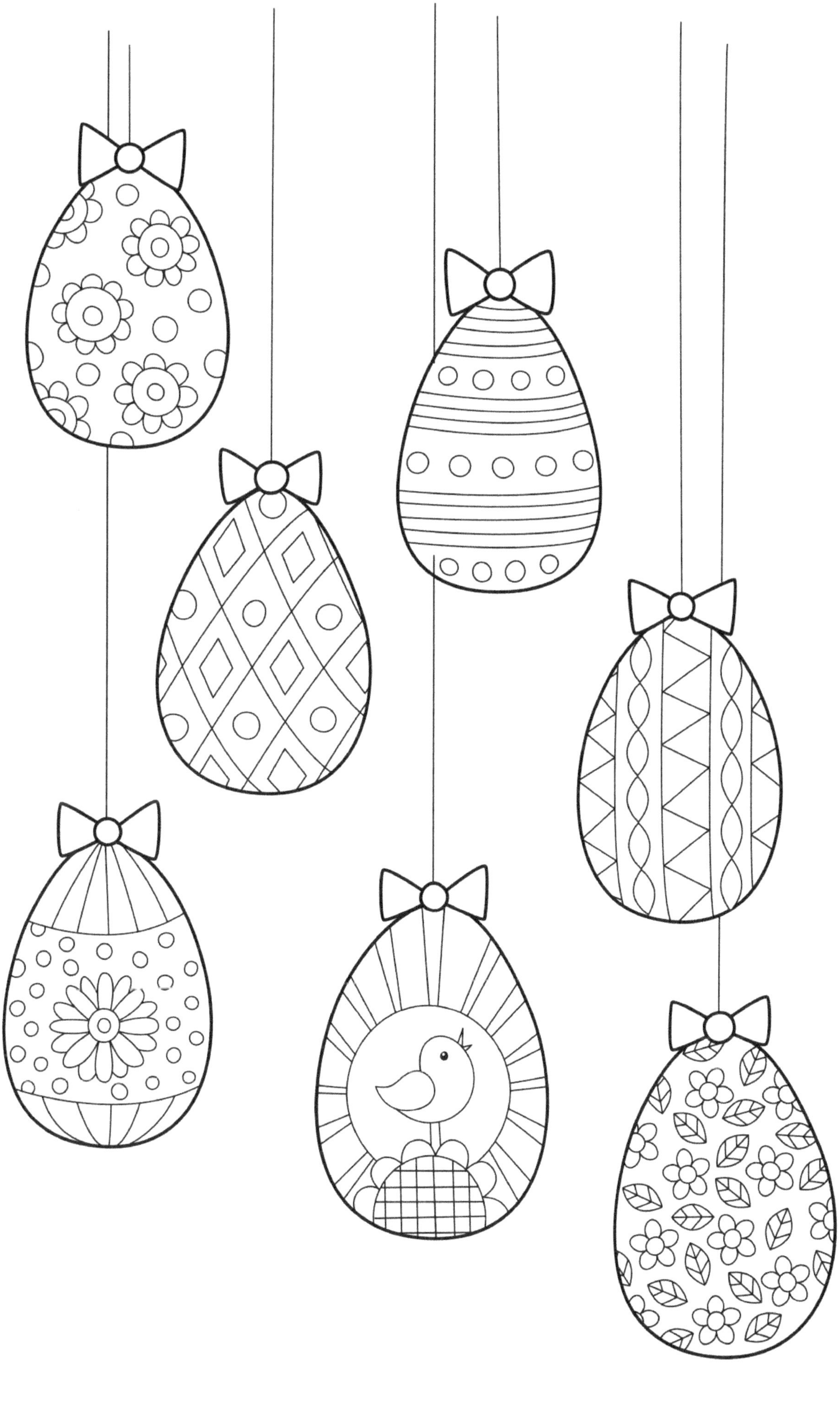

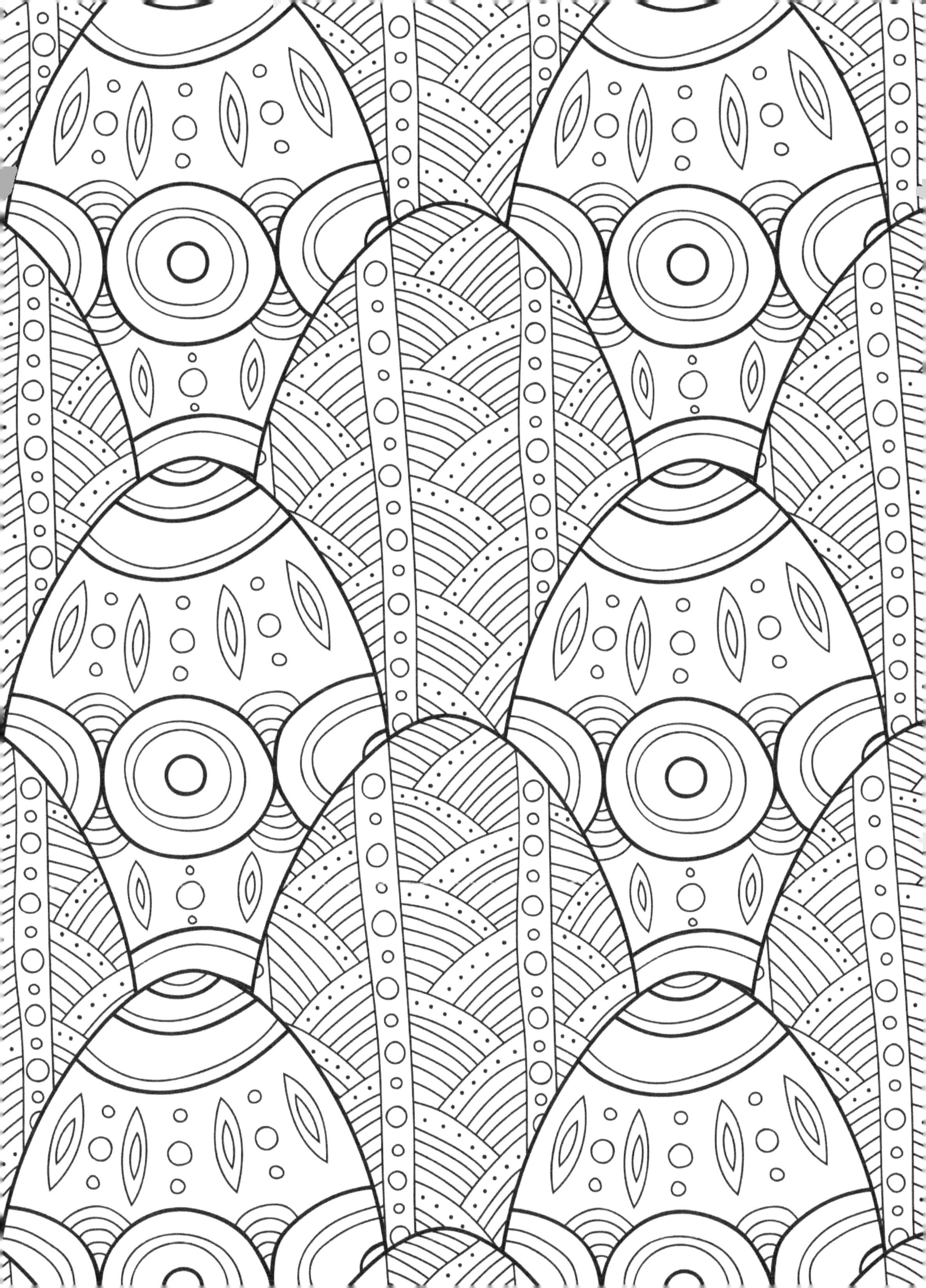

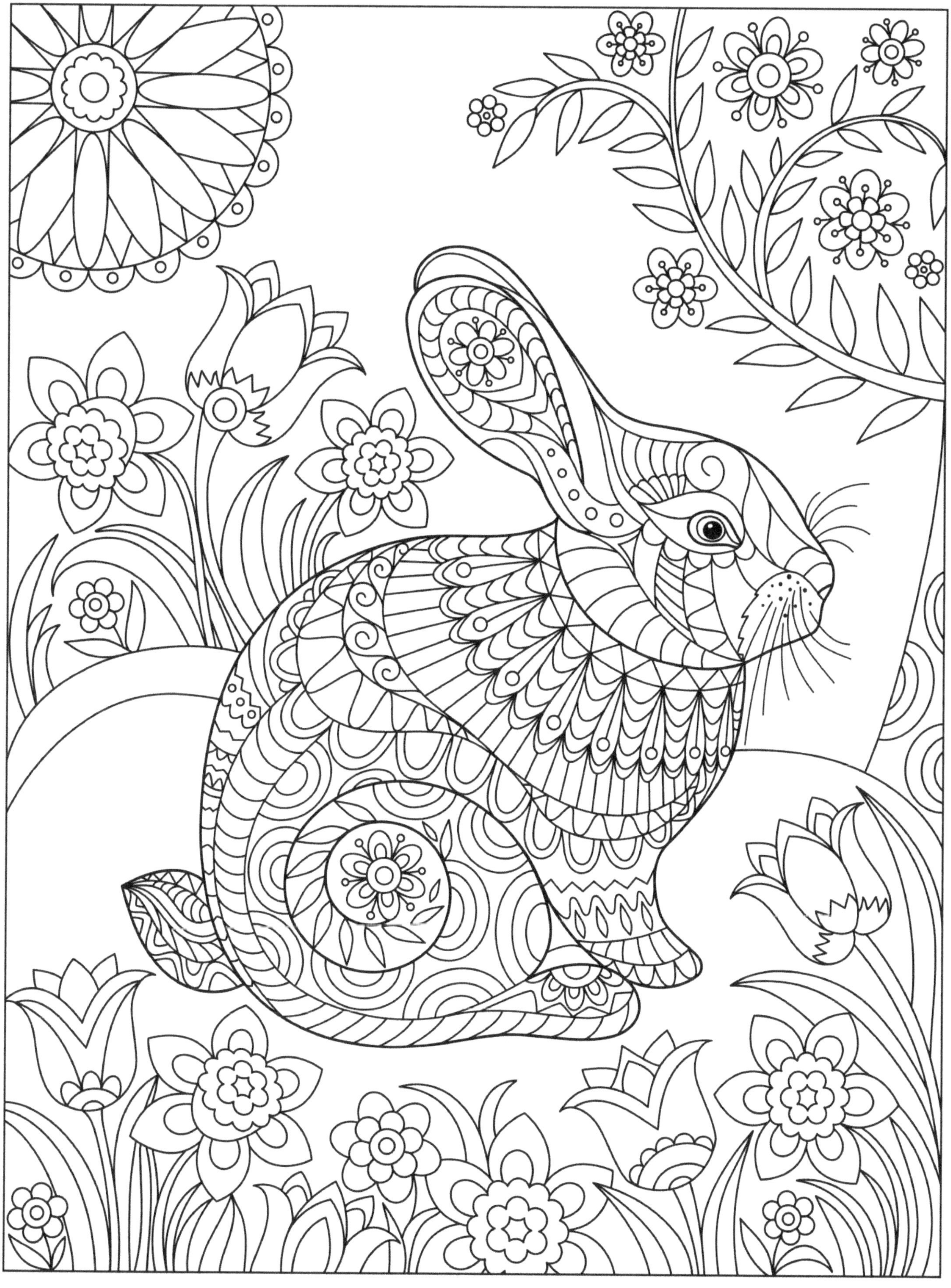

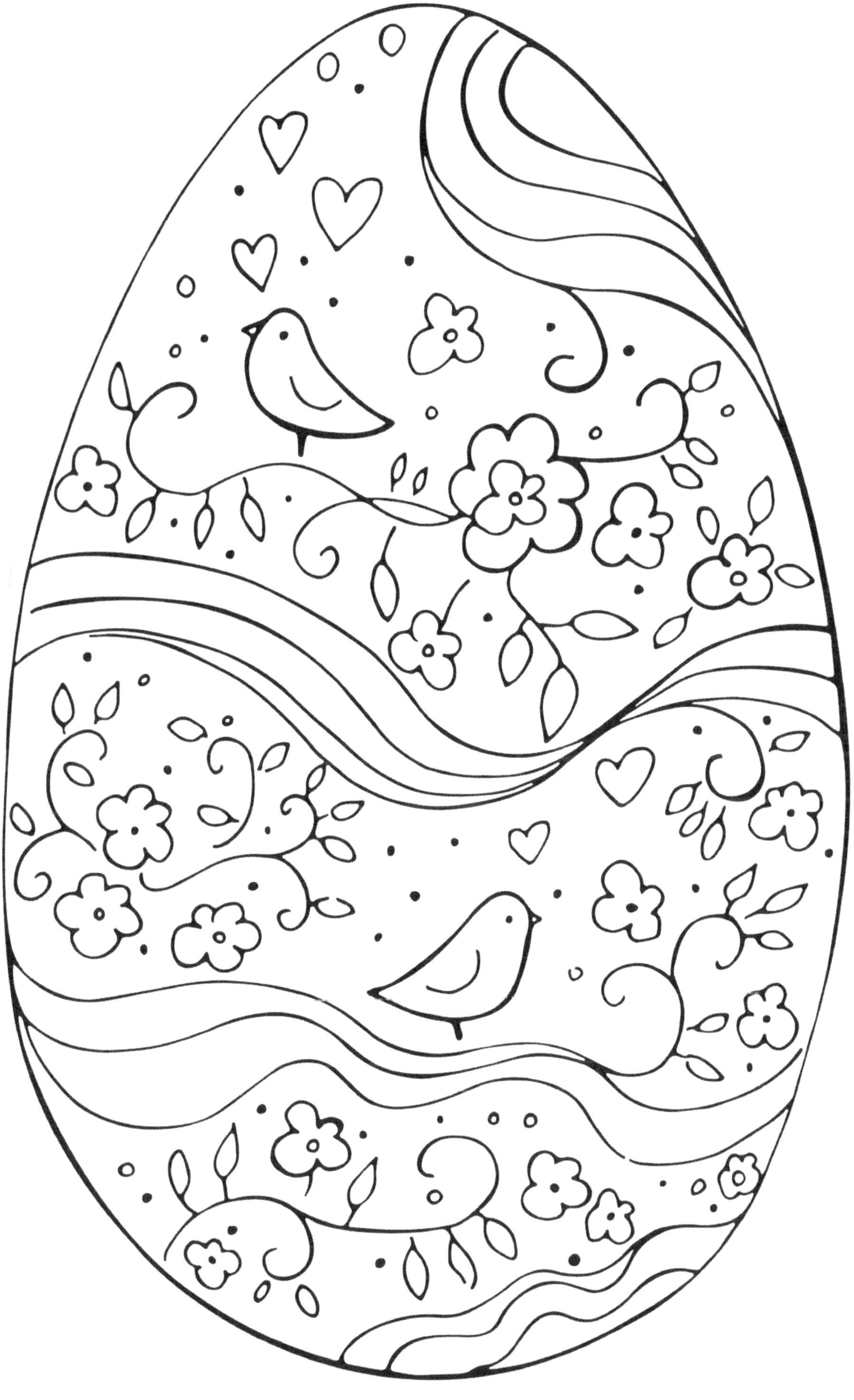

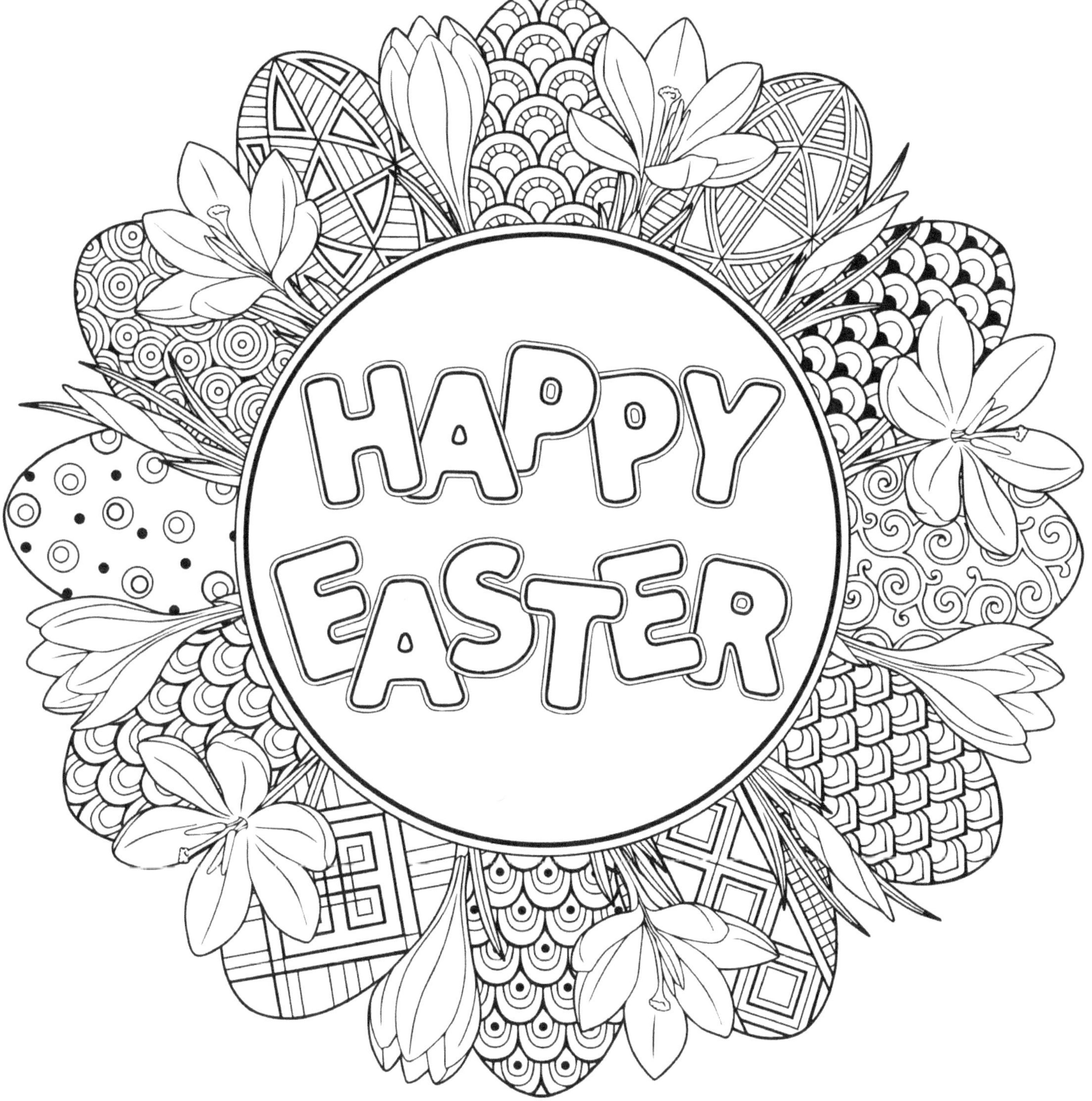
HAPPY
EASTER

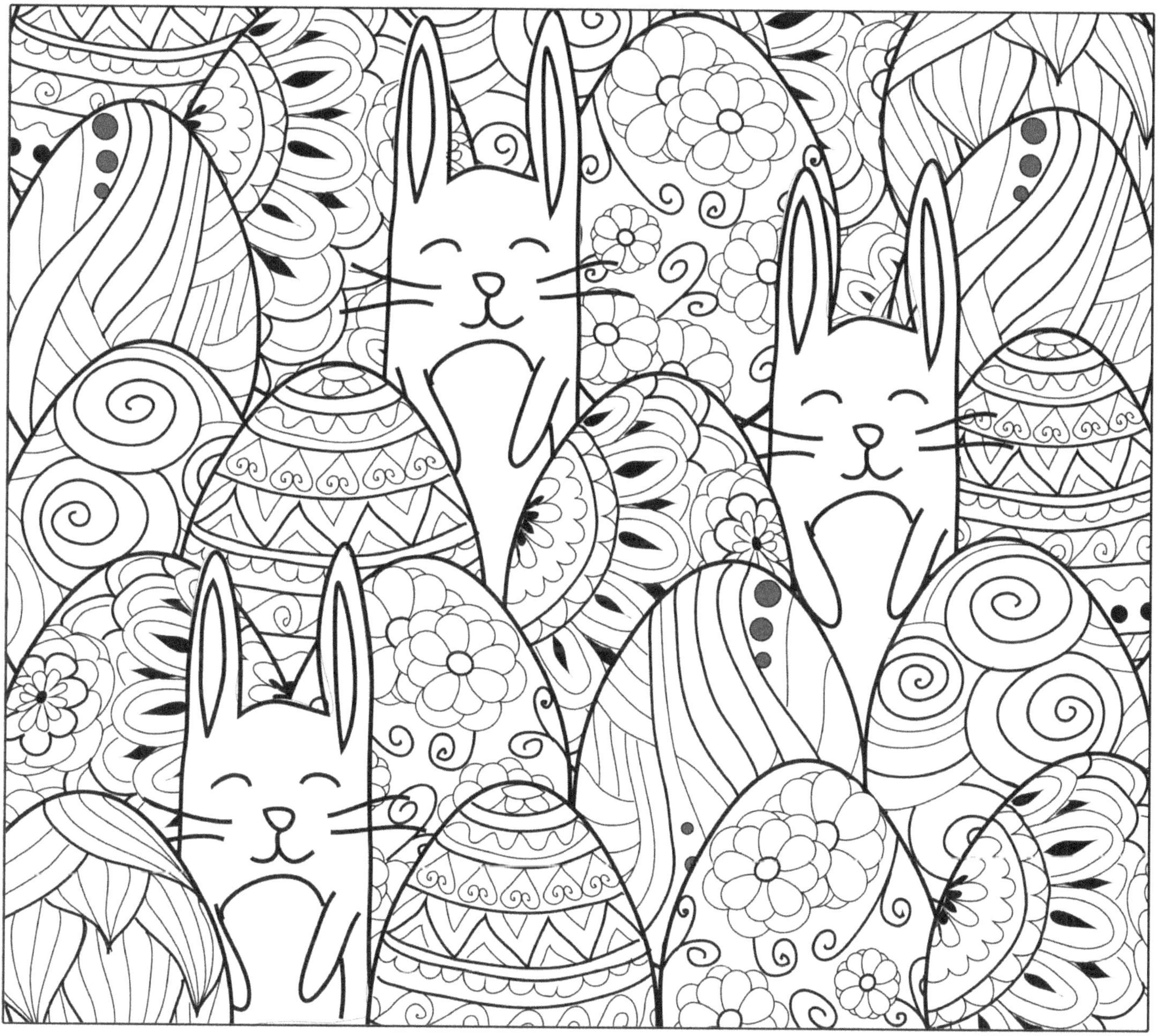

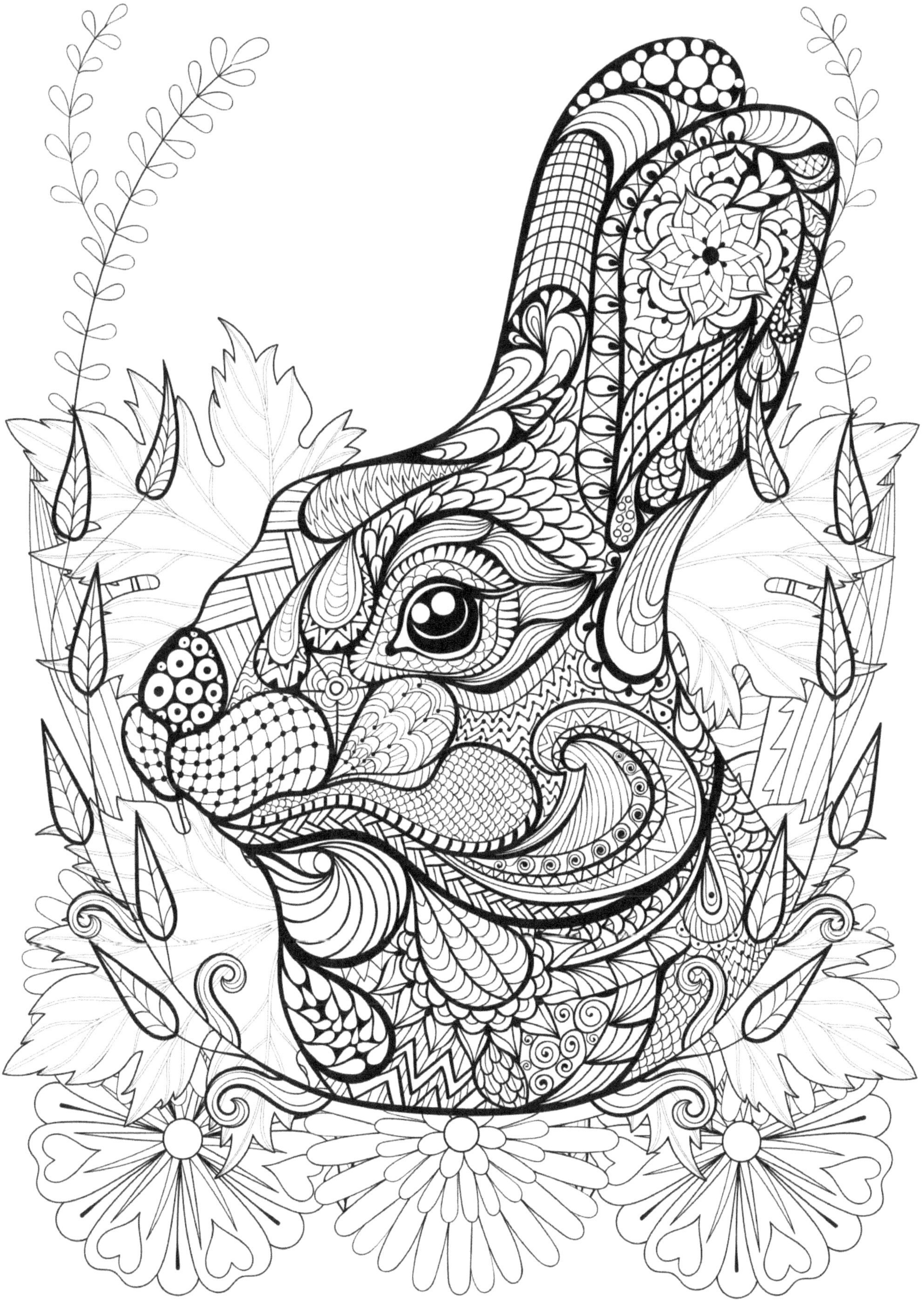

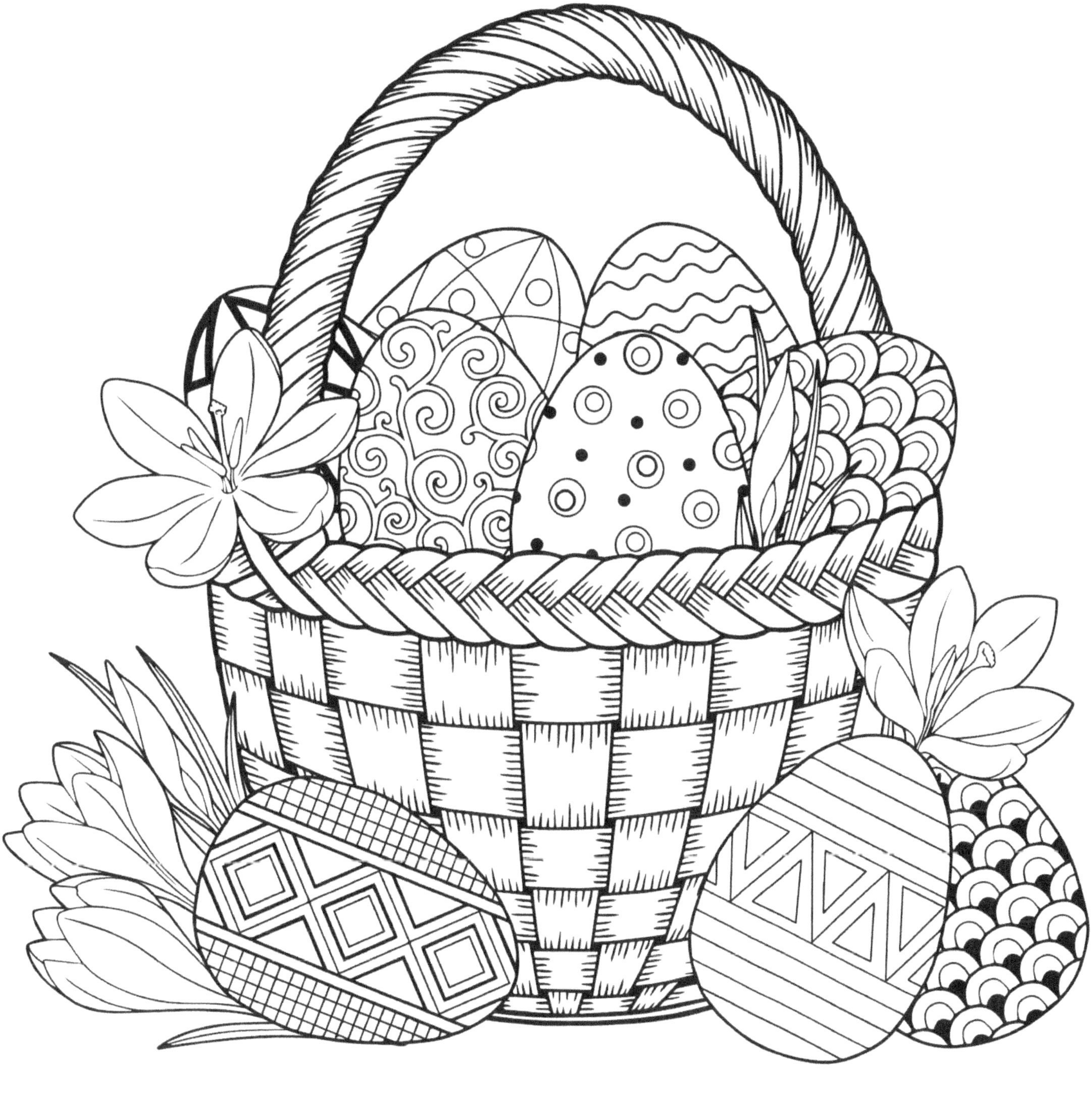

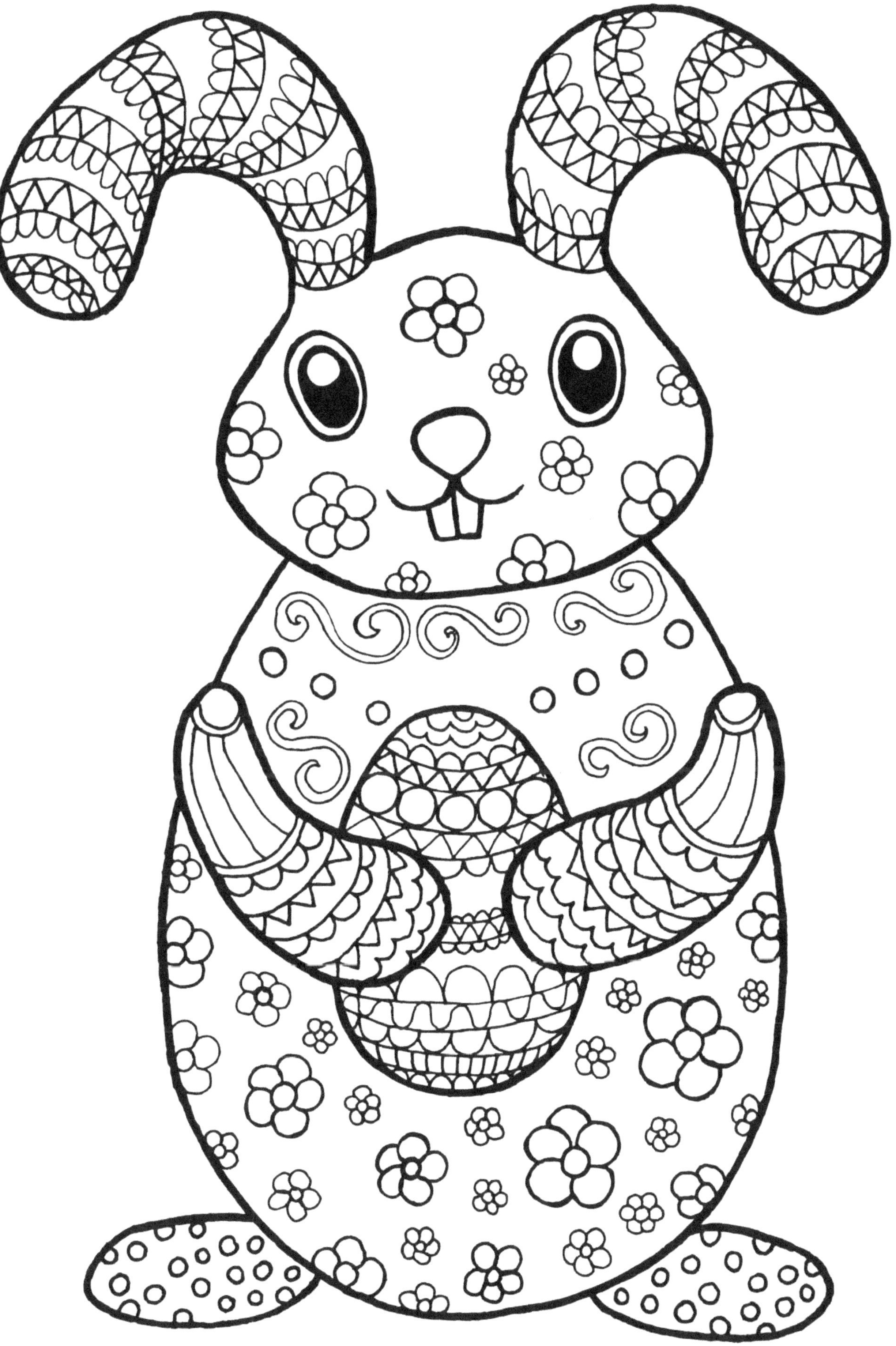

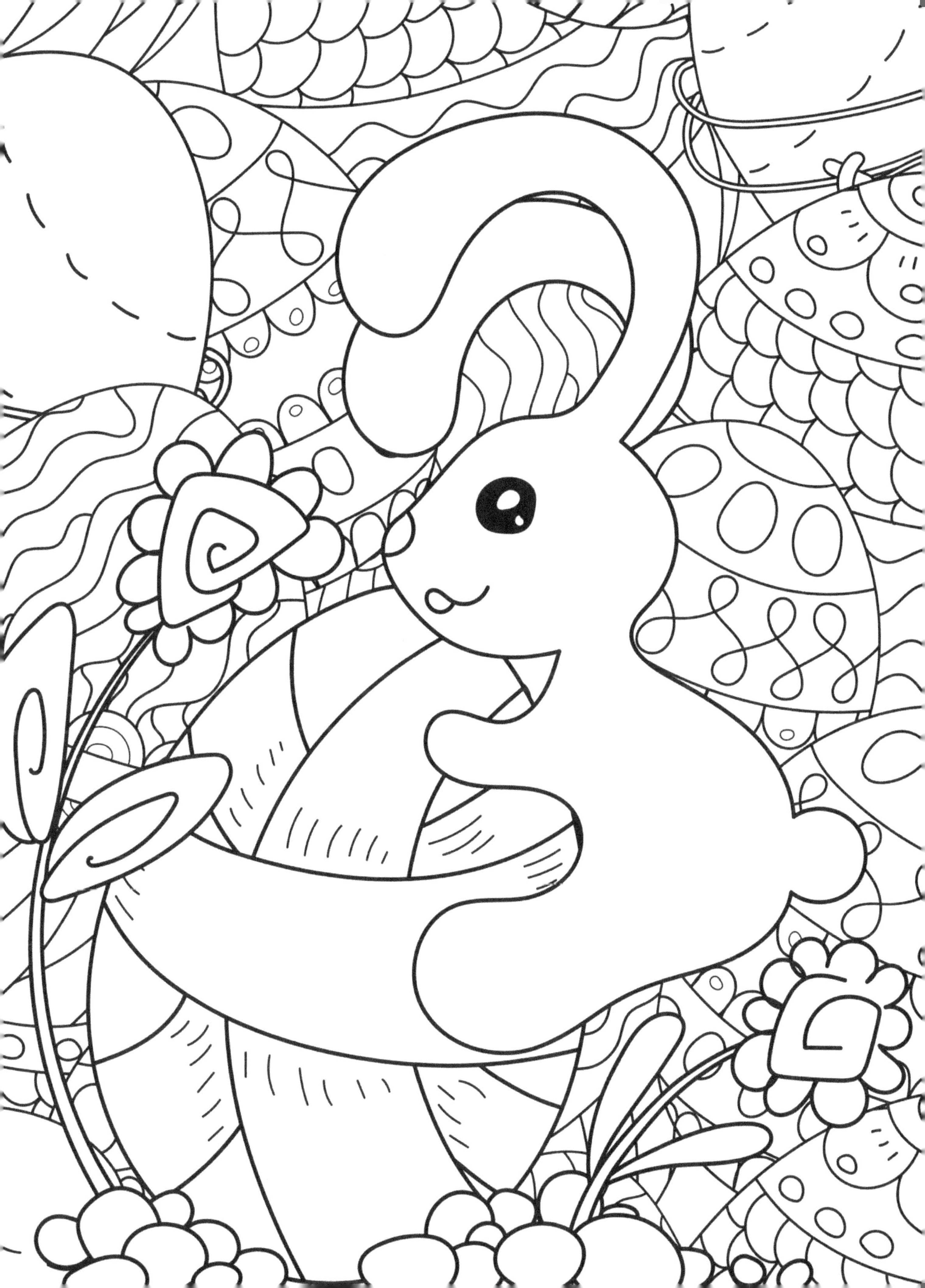

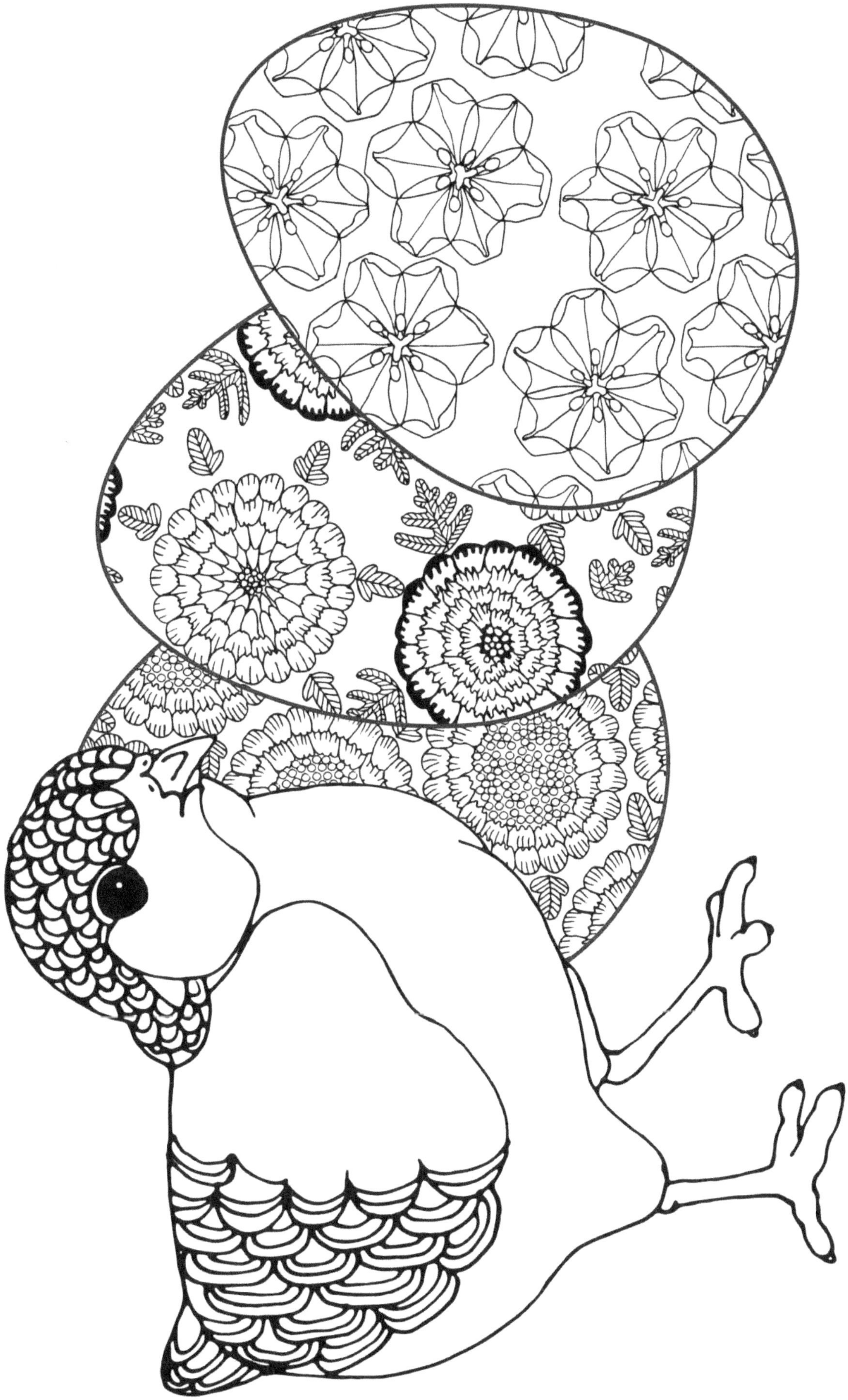

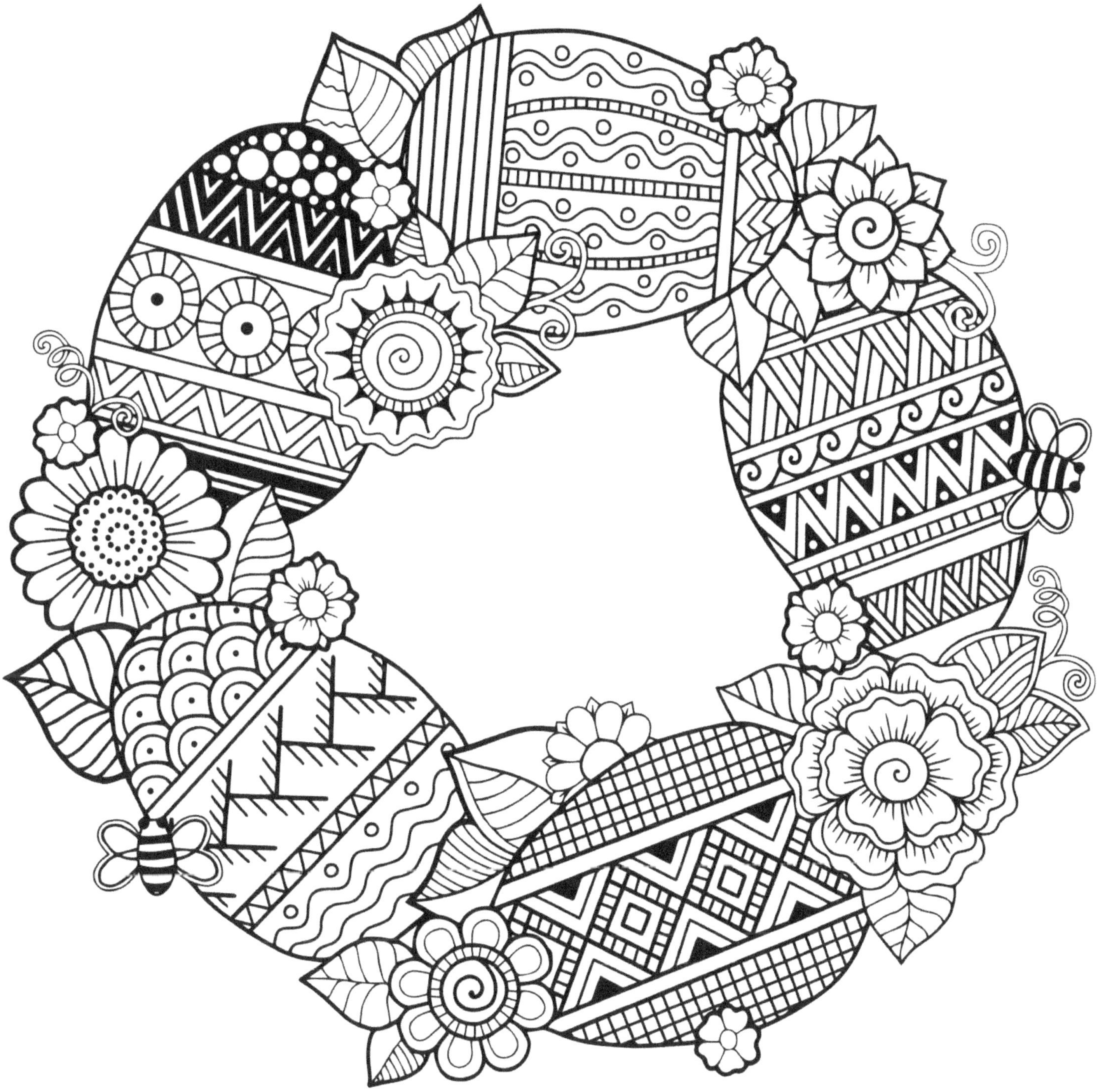

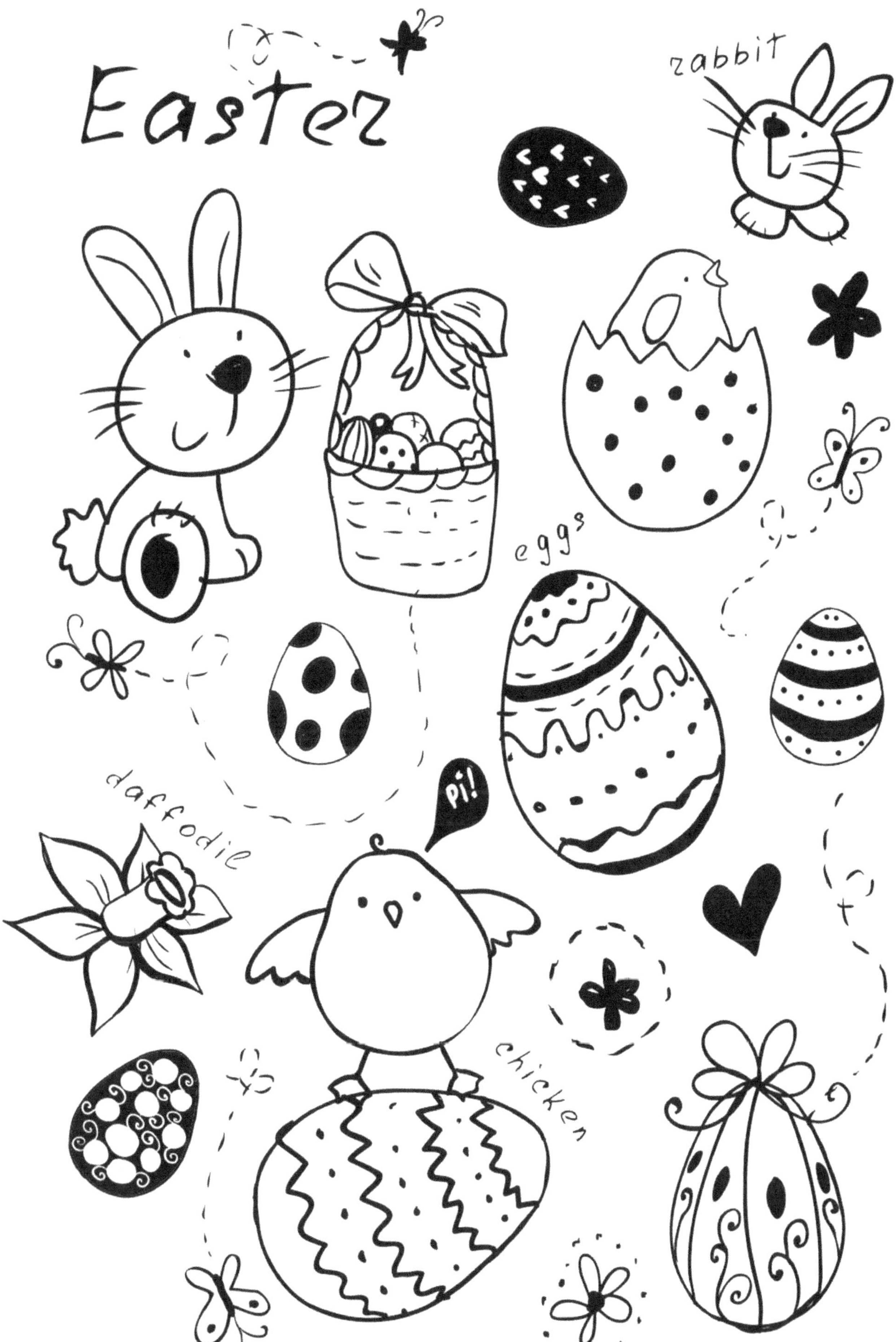
Easter
rabbit
eggs
pi!
daffodil
chicken

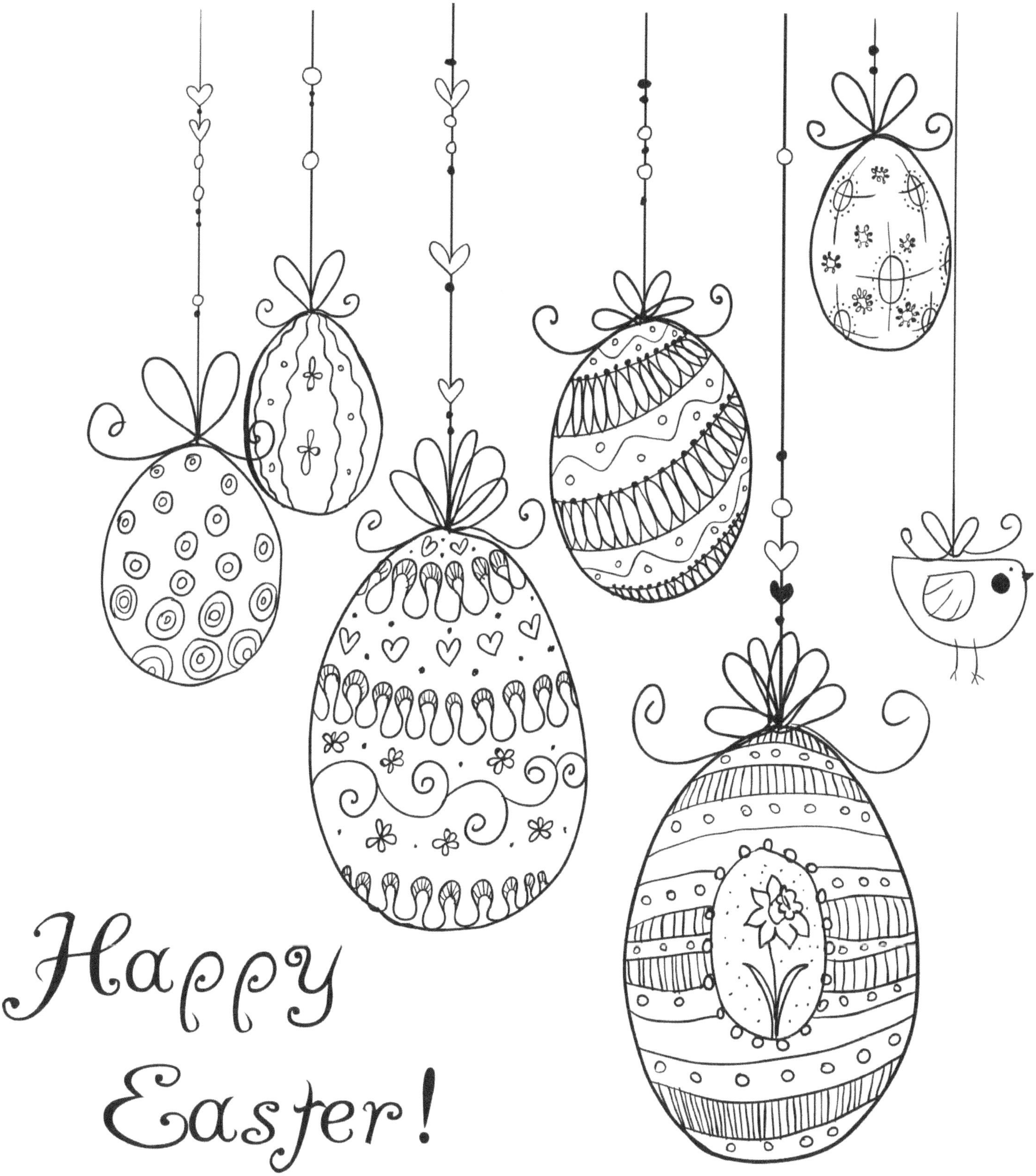
Happy
Easter!

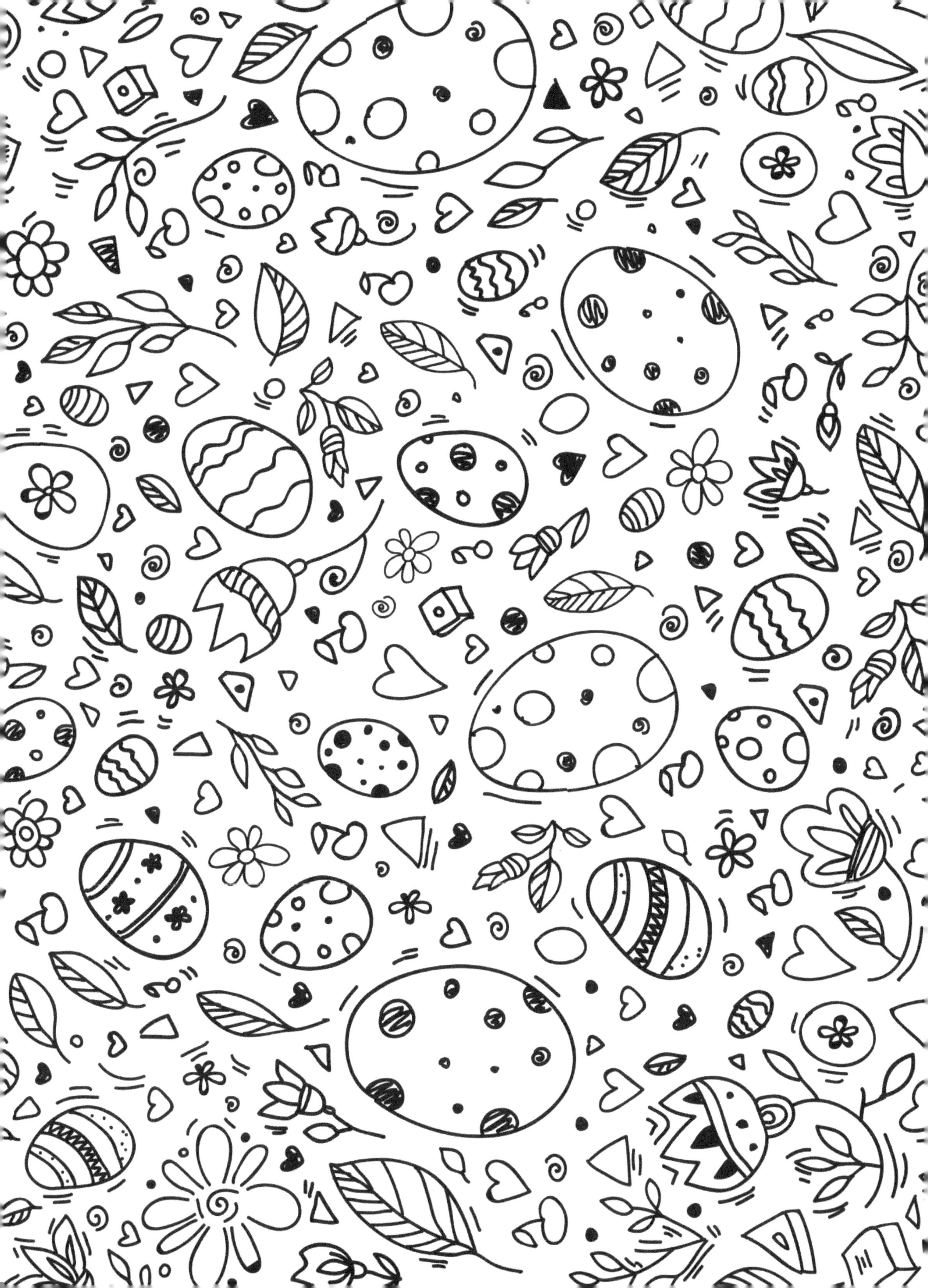

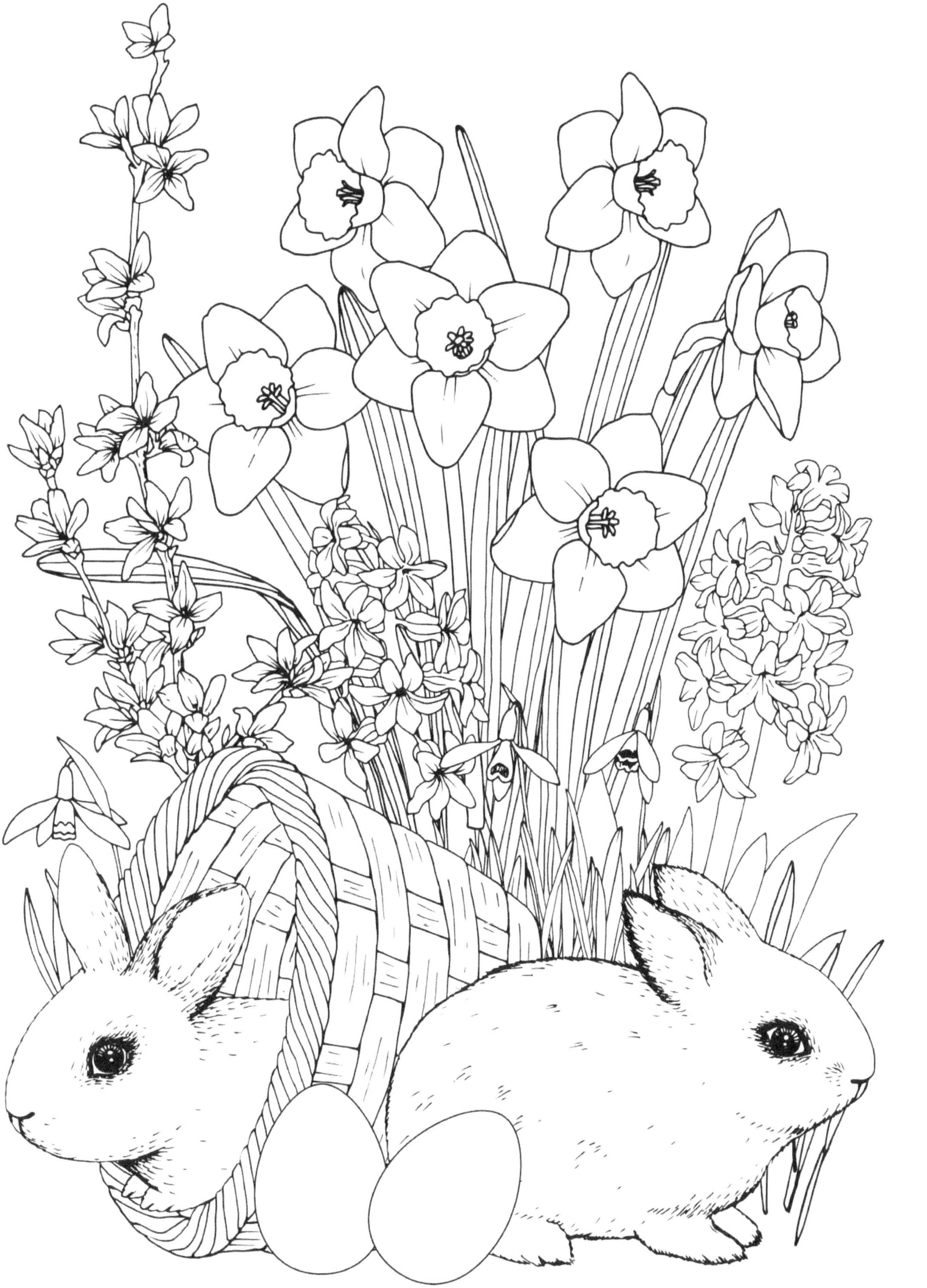

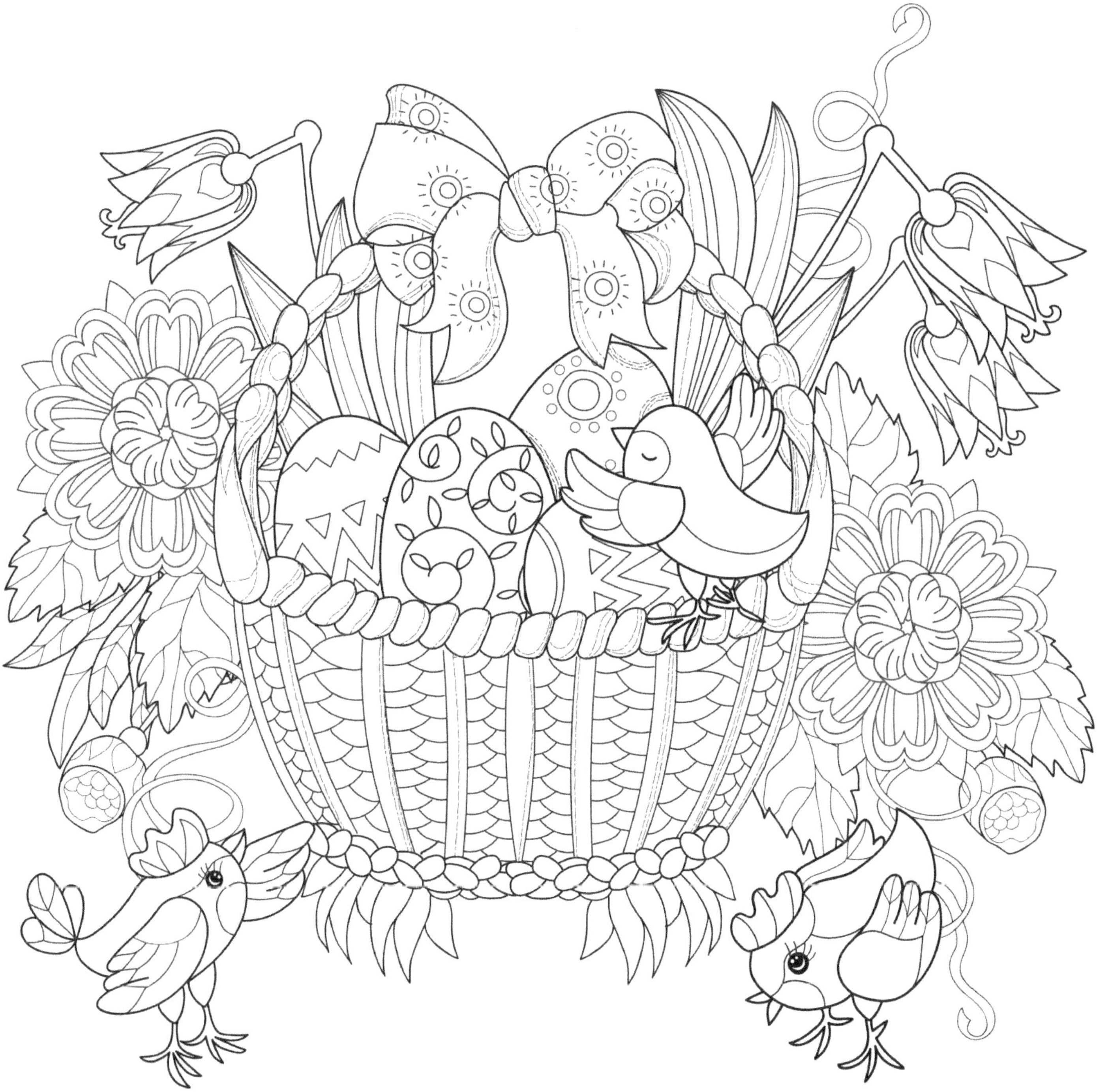

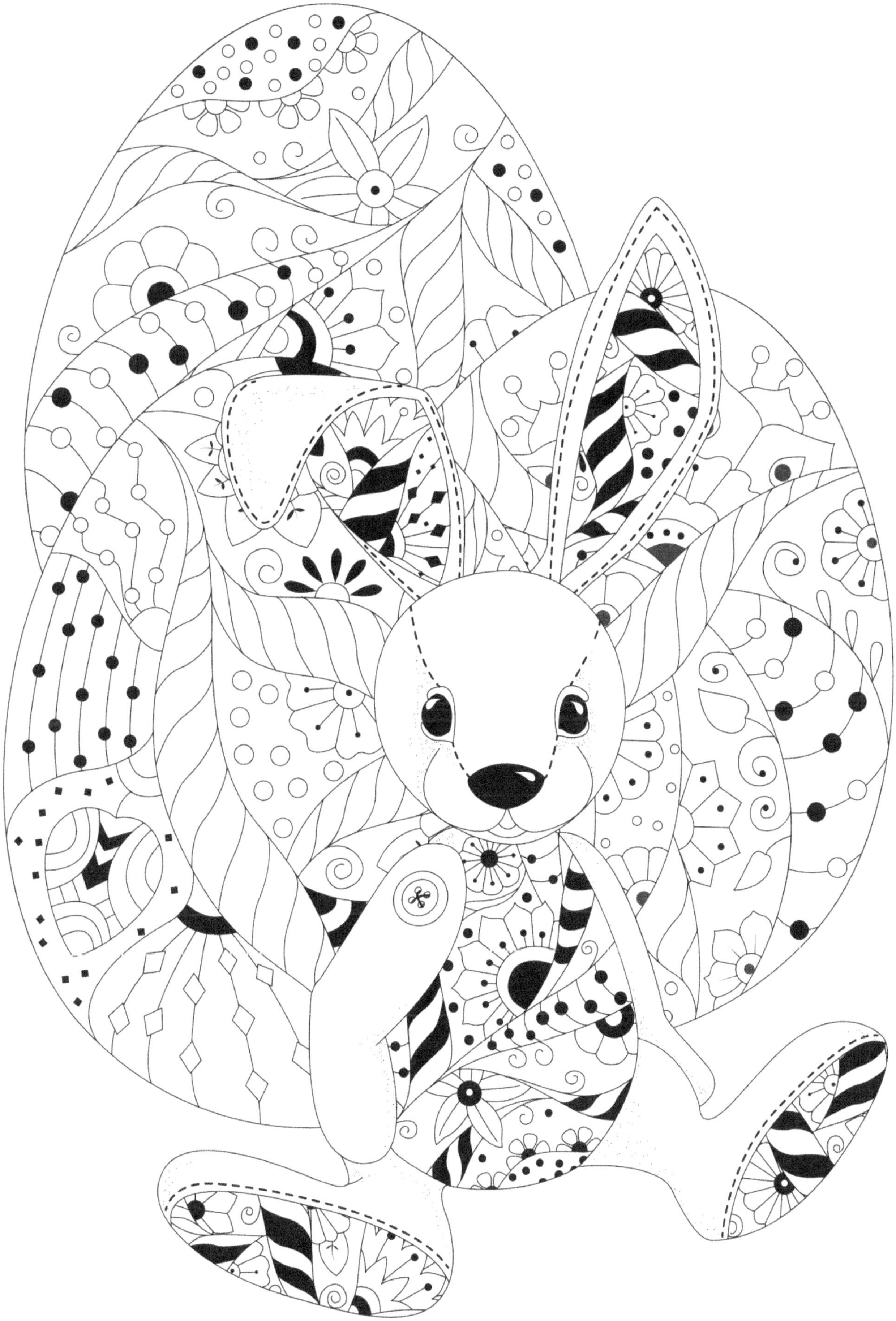

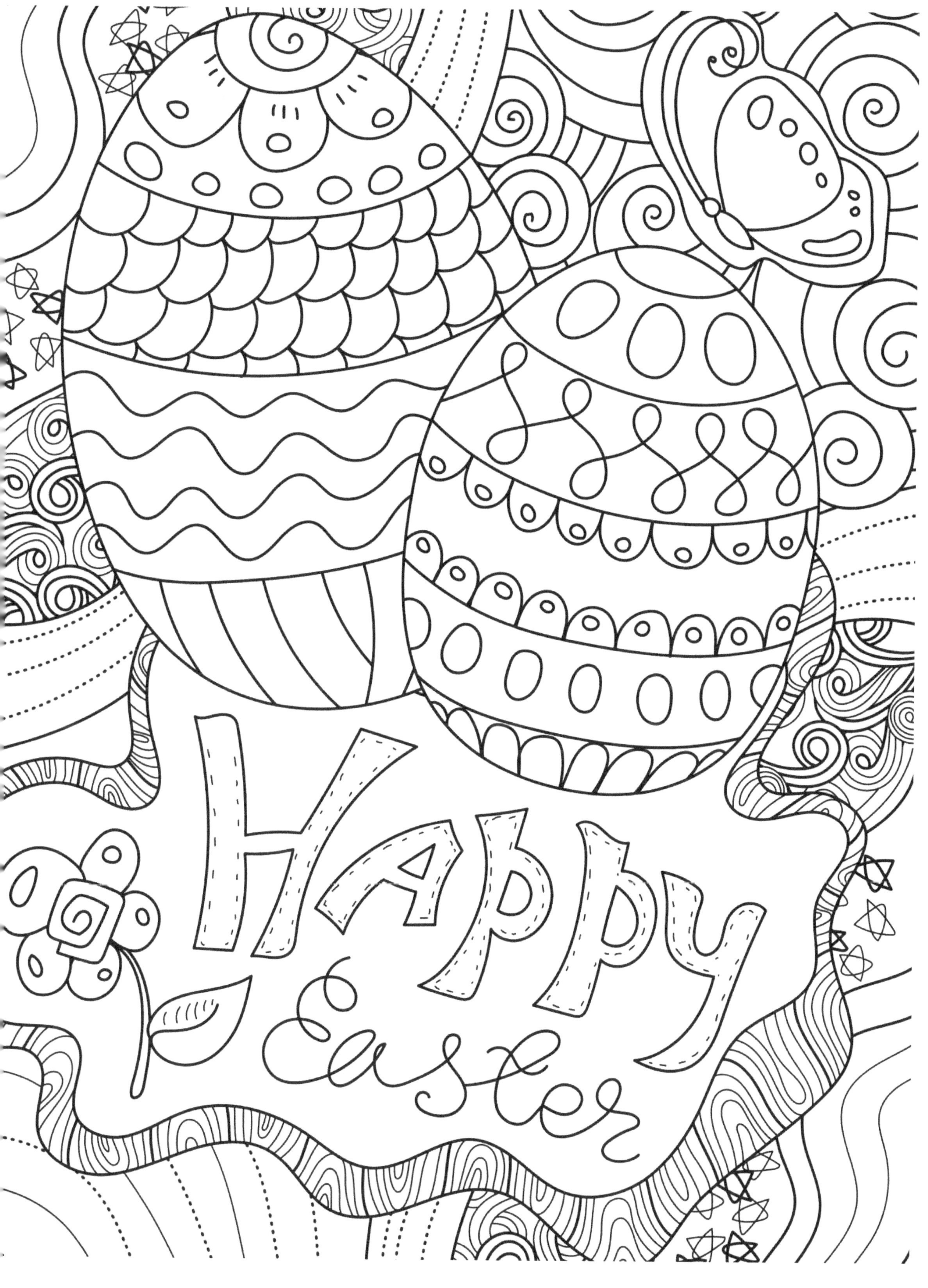
Happy Easter

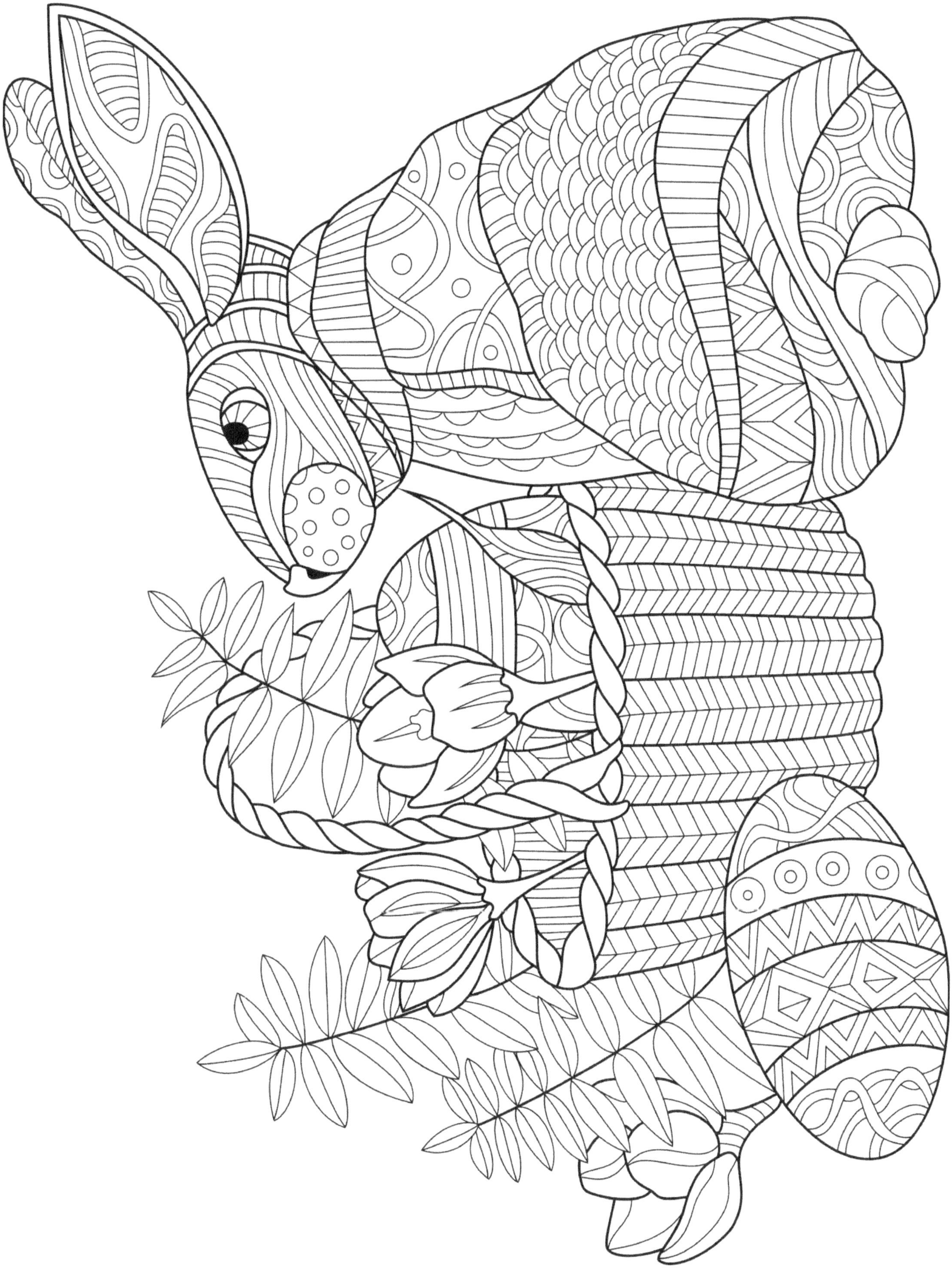

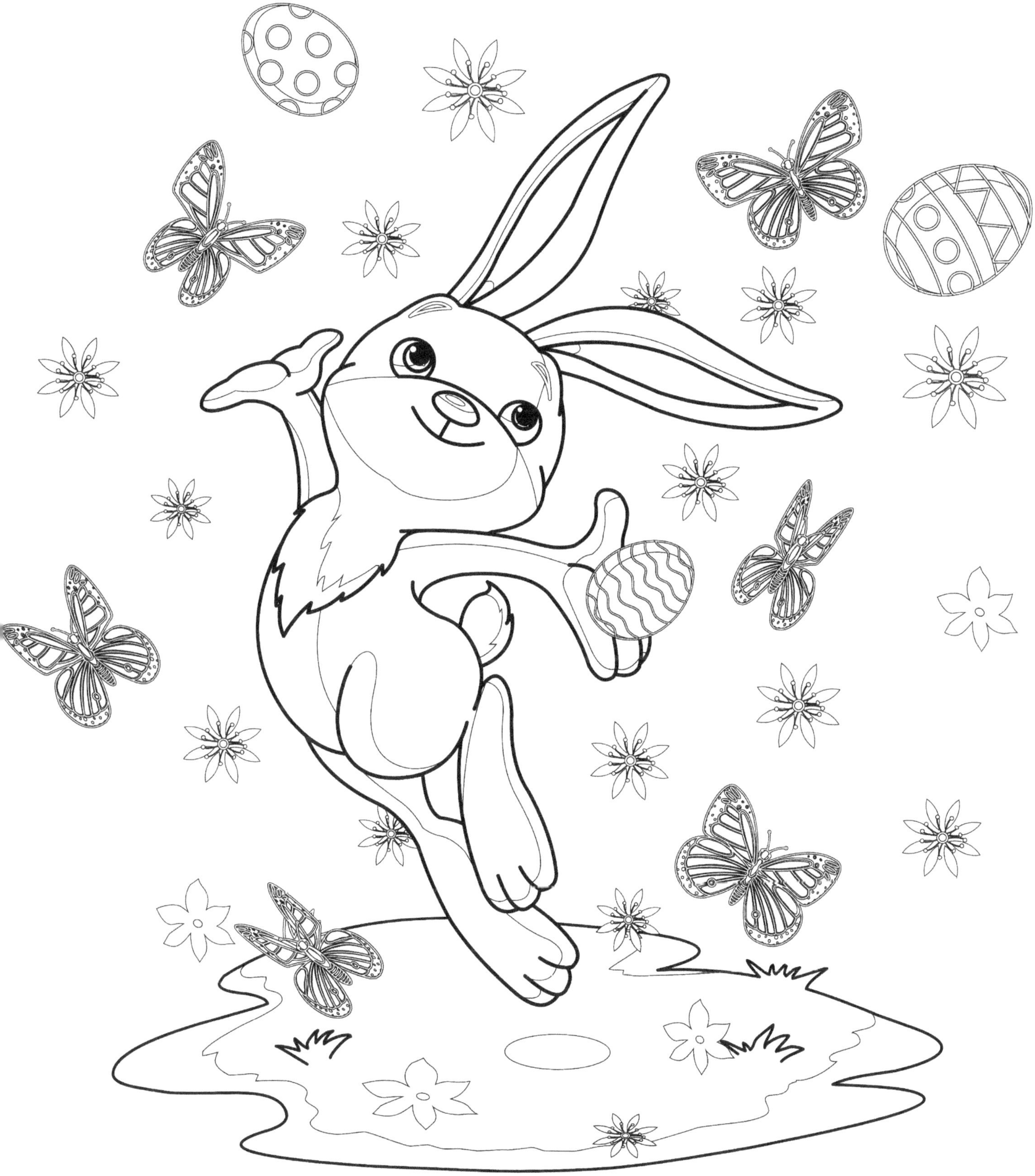

www.ingramcontent.com/pod-product-compliance
Lightning Source LLC
Chambersburg PA
CBHW081018240526
45471CB00017B/3411
9781986197120